# A Love No Less

Also by Pamela Newkirk

*Within the Veil: Black Journalists, White Media*

# A Love No Less

More Than Two Centuries of

African American Love Letters

## Pamela Newkirk

**DOUBLEDAY**

*New York   London   Toronto   Sydney   Auckland*

PUBLISHED BY DOUBLEDAY
a division of Random House, Inc.
1745 Broadway, New York, New York 10019

DOUBLEDAY and the portrayal of an anchor with a dolphin are registered
trademarks of Doubleday, a division of Random House, Inc.

Cataloging-in-Publication Data is on file
with the Library of Congress.
ISBN 0-385-50379-2

PRINTED IN THE UNITED STATES OF AMERICA

February 2003
First Edition
1   2   3   4   5   6   7   8   9   10

*For Michael*

# CONTENTS

PART THREE

## The Harlem Renaissance, the Depression, and a New Deal

PART FOUR

## World War II

PART FIVE

## The Civil Rights Era to the Present

ACKNOWLEDGMENTS

⟋⟍⟋⟍⟍⟋

This book would not be possible without the enthusiasm and guidance of Neeti Madan, an agent extraordinaire who understood and embraced this project from the start, and Janet Hill, whose unbridled passion for this effort was a treasured gift. Thank you both from the bottom of my heart. Every writer should be blessed with such a phenomenal team.

I also am grateful for the many people who were willing to offer tidbits of their family's or their own romantic past; and my father, who fueled my passion for this project early on with his bundle of letters and sepia photographs.

I also appreciate the assistance of the librarians at archives across the country for their assistance. The archives from which the letters have been collected are noted in the text, but it is only fitting to acknowledge in this space the Schomburg Center for Research in Black Culture (with special thanks to Steven G. Fullwood and Diana Lachatanere in the manuscripts division and Anthony Toussaint in the prints division); Howard University Moorland-Spingarn Research Center and its curator Joellen El Bashir; the James Weldon Johnson Collection at Yale University's Beinecke Rare Books and Manuscript Library; the North Carolina State Archives; the Special Collections Division at

Tulane University; the National Archives; the private collections of Lana Turner, who opened her home to me to pore through the letters and photographs from old Harlem that she has lovingly catalogued; and A'Lelia Bundles, who graciously offered a letter from the treasure trove that is her great-grandmother A'Lelia Walker's personal papers. Thanks to all who had the foresight to collect these irreplaceable relics. A special note of appreciation to the late Arthur Schomburg, whose Schomburg Center for Research in Black Culture is a sacred space for any writer interested in African American culture and history.

I've been blessed with a wonderful group of friends whose encouragement spurred me on through periods of uncertainty. I'd particularly like to acknowledge Karen Alexander, Nancy Hass, Onute Miller, Christina Howell Scott, Felicia Lee, and Anita Farrington Brathwaite.

I cannot imagine where I'd be without the constant love and support of my incredible family. Thank you Mommy, Daddy, Dorothy, Tiffany, Barron, and Kamilah. And a kiss to heaven to my late grandparents, Dorothy and Samuel Spencer, whose lifelong commitment to each other continues to inspire me. And no words seem adequate to convey my appreciation for the sustained support of my husband Michael and my darling angels—Marjani, Mykel, and Stacey.

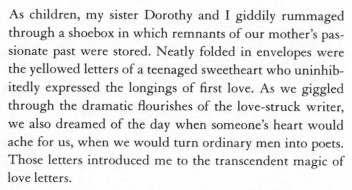

As children, my sister Dorothy and I giddily rummaged through a shoebox in which remnants of our mother's passionate past were stored. Neatly folded in envelopes were the yellowed letters of a teenaged sweetheart who uninhibitedly expressed the longings of first love. As we giggled through the dramatic flourishes of the love-struck writer, we also dreamed of the day when someone's heart would ache for us, when we would turn ordinary men into poets. Those letters introduced me to the transcendent magic of love letters.

Love letters are, by their very nature, intensely private. To read the love letters of others is to eavesdrop on the most heartfelt of exchanges. This collection allows us to partake in an otherwise forbidden pursuit, offering us rare glimpses of the emotional lives of private and public figures alike. These letters make soul mates of strangers while they demystify and reveal as poignantly vulnerable some of the larger-than-life public personalities from the past—from civil rights leader Mary Church Terrell to James Weldon

Johnson. Many of the letters in this collection are decorously penned by hand, accentuating their intimacy and distinctiveness. At a time when many of our exchanges transpire over the Internet or by cell phone, these letters recall a time when letters were lovingly crafted by the writer, and eagerly anticipated and savored by the recipient. We are reminded that love letter–writing may, in fact, be a dying art. Still, these letters—which span more than two centuries—capture a timeless, primal, and universal emotion. As we review these relics of passion, we are connected to our shared humanity—to our highest calling as humans.

The idea for this collection grew both out of my passion for history and letters, and by the void in popular literature of love letters written by African Americans. We know African Americans have sung the blues, have marched against injustice, and have turned to God in the face of oppression. We know that some have soared in the arts, business, and sports while others have been bowed and broken by the weight of adversity. But, through it all, African Americans have loved, and they have done so in ways no less pure and marvelous than others. This book is a testament to the love that has survived the hardships of slavery, war, discrimination, and poverty.

Some of the letters in this volume were written by or to celebrated African Americans like turn-of-the-century poet Paul Laurence Dunbar; 1930s screen legend Fredi Washington; Harlem Renaissance writers James Weldon Johnson and Countee Cullen; and civil rights leader Mary Church Terrell. Others were written by lesser-known African Americans from diverse backgrounds—including slaves, soldiers, and surgeons. We are introduced to figures

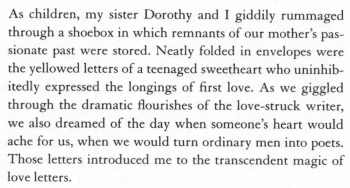

As children, my sister Dorothy and I giddily rummaged through a shoebox in which remnants of our mother's passionate past were stored. Neatly folded in envelopes were the yellowed letters of a teenaged sweetheart who uninhibitedly expressed the longings of first love. As we giggled through the dramatic flourishes of the love-struck writer, we also dreamed of the day when someone's heart would ache for us, when we would turn ordinary men into poets. Those letters introduced me to the transcendent magic of love letters.

Love letters are, by their very nature, intensely private. To read the love letters of others is to eavesdrop on the most heartfelt of exchanges. This collection allows us to partake in an otherwise forbidden pursuit, offering us rare glimpses of the emotional lives of private and public figures alike. These letters make soul mates of strangers while they demystify and reveal as poignantly vulnerable some of the larger-than-life public personalities from the past—from civil rights leader Mary Church Terrell to James Weldon

Johnson. Many of the letters in this collection are decorously penned by hand, accentuating their intimacy and distinctiveness. At a time when many of our exchanges transpire over the Internet or by cell phone, these letters recall a time when letters were lovingly crafted by the writer, and eagerly anticipated and savored by the recipient. We are reminded that love letter–writing may, in fact, be a dying art. Still, these letters—which span more than two centuries—capture a timeless, primal, and universal emotion. As we review these relics of passion, we are connected to our shared humanity—to our highest calling as humans.

The idea for this collection grew both out of my passion for history and letters, and by the void in popular literature of love letters written by African Americans. We know African Americans have sung the blues, have marched against injustice, and have turned to God in the face of oppression. We know that some have soared in the arts, business, and sports while others have been bowed and broken by the weight of adversity. But, through it all, African Americans have loved, and they have done so in ways no less pure and marvelous than others. This book is a testament to the love that has survived the hardships of slavery, war, discrimination, and poverty.

Some of the letters in this volume were written by or to celebrated African Americans like turn-of-the-century poet Paul Laurence Dunbar; 1930s screen legend Fredi Washington; Harlem Renaissance writers James Weldon Johnson and Countee Cullen; and civil rights leader Mary Church Terrell. Others were written by lesser-known African Americans from diverse backgrounds—including slaves, soldiers, and surgeons. We are introduced to figures from the early 1900s like the Grangers: Dr. Isabella Granger was a gynecologist, and her husband, Dr. William Randolph Granger, Jr., hailed from a family of prominent physicians. Reading their letters highlights the challenges of two-career, commuter marriages, preceding by half a century the Women's Rights Movement. One may also be struck by the surprisingly modern and feminist stance of letter writers like Roscoe Conkling Bruce, who in 1903 tells his beloved that he wants her to be his full partner in all things, including intellectual pursuits.

By reading the love letters of slaves, we experience their pain of separation as they contemplate ways to reunite with their spouses, or as they become resigned to their torturous fates apart.

Through these letters—gleaned from dusty attics, photo albums, and archives across the country—we bear witness to the love that has sustained African Americans throughout their turbulent history in America. While this aspect of African American life is underrepresented in mainstream culture, this collection is a tribute to its divine and enduring presence through the ages.

## PART ONE

# The Nineteenth Century

## Slavery, Emancipation, Reconstruction, and Retrenchment

### 1858 *to* 1899

F ALL OF THE LETTERS in this volume, the most bittersweet are those written by slaves to the partners from whom they've been separated. These letters concretely demonstrate the persistence of African Americans in maintaining some semblance of family despite the unnatural constrictions imposed by slavery. In two of the letters that follow, the husbands speak of reuniting with their wives in heaven if not on earth. These letters are rare due to the inability of many African American families to maintain their belongings, the limited ability of slaves to write, and the even more difficult task of having letters written by or to slaves successfully delivered to their intended destinations. Compounding this was, for many years, the diminutive value accorded the historical relics of black American life.

While many slave letters were published in abolitionist newspapers, the original copies were often destroyed, leaving only transcribed remains. Still, some of these letters have been compiled in several important books, among them *Slave Testimony: Two Centuries of Letters, Speeches, Interviews and Autobiographies,* by the late John W. Blassingame, and *Free At Last: A Documentary History of Slavery, Freedom and the Civil War,* edited by Ira Berlin, Barbara J. Fields, Steven F. Miller, Joseph P. Reidy, and Leslie S. Rowland. As Blassingame notes in *Slave Testimony,* the best source of slave testimony are the letters written by slaves to their families. "There is no false modesty intended for the eyes of masters or bravado to impress white abolitionists," he writes. "Instead, these letters represent a baring of the soul intended only for the eyes of loved ones."

The letters written by slaves are followed by those written by recently emancipated African Americans, some of whom achieved major success in business, politics, and the arts. The years following emancipation ushered in a period of extraordinary African American achievement, including the election of blacks to legislative office. In Massachusetts alone, Edward G. Walker and Charles L. Mitchell were elected to the Massachusetts House of Representatives in 1866.

In 1867, Congress passed a series of Reconstruction Acts as well as the Fourteenth Amendment to ensure African American political participation in the South. That year saw the opening of Howard University and what is now Morehouse College. A year later, Hampton Institute opened in Virginia. In 1868, the Fourteenth Amendment, by making all persons born or naturalized in the United States citizens, gave constitutional guarantees to African Americans. That year, during the meeting of the South Carolina Legislature in Columbia, more than half of the lawmakers were black, making South Carolina the only state legislature in American history to have a black majority. Alonzo J. Ransier, an African American, was lieutenant governor in 1870, followed by Richard H. Gleaves in 1872. Two African Americans, Samuel J. Lee and Robert B. Elliot, served as Speaker of the House between 1872 and 1874. Francis L. Cardozo served as secretary of state from 1868 to 1872 and state treasurer from 1872 to 1876.

In 1870, Jonathan Jasper Wright of Pennsylvania became associate justice of the South Carolina Supreme Court, a position he held for seven years. That same year, Hiram R. Revels of Mississippi took Jefferson Davis's seat in the U.S. Senate, becoming the lone black in the U.S. Congress.

In 1870, Richard T. Greener was the first black graduate of Harvard University, and a year later, Father Patrick Francis Healy, a black priest, became president of Georgetown University. In 1872, P. B. S. Pinchback, a former Union officer and lieutenant governor of Louisiana, was named temporary governor of the state, a position he held for forty-three days. And in 1875, Blanche Kelso Bruce—whose son's letters are included in this volume—became Mississippi's second black senator and the first African American to serve a full term in the U.S. Senate. In 1876, Meharry Medical College, the first black medical school in the United States, was established in Nashville, Tennessee.

But a fierce backlash against advances by blacks finally resulted in an 1883 U.S. Supreme Court ruling that the Civil Rights Act of 1875 was unconstitutional. Other measures followed, including Black Codes that enforced racial segregation and the political disenfranchisement of blacks.

In 1896, there were 130,344 registered black voters in Louisiana, but by 1900, two years after a new constitution was adopted, there were 5,320.

More than 2,500 African Americans were reported lynched during the last sixteen years of the nineteenth century, with Mississippi, Alabama, Georgia, and Louisiana leading the nation.

Still, with the exception of the heartbreaking letters written by slaves forcibly separated from their loved ones, few of these letters bear traces of the hardships African Americans endured during those turbulent times. Instead, many poetically express the ecstasy and yearning of love.

The letter by Abream Scriven, like the others written by slaves that follow, is presented as written, without correcting grammatical and spelling errors. What these letters reveal is the devastating impact forced separation had on slaves who had somehow managed to build strong family lives.

## ABREAM SCRIVEN TO DINAH JONES

*September 19, 1858*

*From the Charles Colcock Jones Papers, Special
Collections Division, Tulane University*

My Dear Wife,

I take the pleasure of writing you these few with
much regret to inform you that I am sold to a man
by the name of Peterson atreader and Stays in new
orleans. I am here yet But I expect to go before long
but when I get there I will write and let you know
where I am. My Dear I want to Send you some
things but I donot know who to Send them by but
I will thry to get them to you and my children.
Give my love to my father and mother and tell them
good Bye for me. and if we Shall not meet in this
world I hope to meet in heaven. My Dear wife for
you and my children my pen cannot Express the
griffe I feel to be parted from you all

I remain your truly husband until death
Abream Scriven

Paris Mo Jany

78

My Dear Husband

I recd y

dated Jany 9th also

dated Jany 1st but ha

no one till now to wr

_____ you do not kn

had I am treated

are treating me wo

worse every day. C

cris for you. Send

money as soon as y

for me and Mary th

almost naked. My c

in the cown and a

is telling then i

out. Do not sen

your letters to

## ANN, A MISSOURI SLAVE, TO
## ANDREW VALENTINE, HER SOLDIER HUSBAND

*January 19, 1864 from Paris, Missouri*

National Archives, Enclosed in Brig. General William A. Pile
to Major O. D. Greene, Feb. 11, 1864

My Dear Husband,

I r'ecd your letter dated Jan. 9th also one dated Jan'y
1st but have got no one till now to write for me.
You do not know how bad I am treated. They are
treating me worse and worse every day. Our child
cries for you. Send me some money as soon as you
can for me and my child are almost naked. My cloth
is yet in the loom and there is no telling when it will
be out. Do not send any of your letters to Hogsett
especially those having money in them as Hogsett
will keep the money. George Combs went to
Hannibal soon after you did so I did not get that
money from him. Do the best you can and do not
fret too much for me for it wont be long before I
will be free and then all we make will be ours.

> Your affectionate wife,
> Ann

P.S. Send our little girl a string of beads in your next
letter to remember you by. Ann

## John Boston to His Wife Elizabeth

*January 12, 1862*

National Archives

My Dear Wife it is with great joy I take this time to
let you know Whare I am I am now in Safety in the
14th Regiment of Brooklyn this Day I can Adress
you thank god as a free man. I had a little truble in
giting away But as the lord led the Children of Isrel
to the land of Canon So he led me to a land Whare
freedom Will rain in spite Of earth and hell Dear
you must make your Self content I am free from the
Slavers Lash and as you have chose the Wise plan
Of Serving the lord I hope you Will pray Much and
I Will try by the help of god To Serv him With all
my hart I am With a very nice man and have All
that hart Can Wish But My Dear I Cant express my
grate desire that I Have to See you I trust the time
Will Come When We Shal meet again And if We
don't met on eart We Will Meet in heven Whare
Jesas ranes Dear Elizabeth tell Mrs. Own That I
trust that She Will Continue Her kindness to you
and that god Will Bless her on earth and Save her
In grate eternity. My accmplements To Mrs. Owens
and her Children may They Prosper through life

I never Shall forgit her kindness to me Dear
Wife I must Close rest yourself Contented I am
free I Want you to rite To me Soon as you Can
Without Delay Direct your letter to the 14th
Regiment new york State malitia Uptons Hill
Virginea In Care of M' Crannford

———ᴥᴥᴥ———

# Nicey Moore and Harvey

*From Howard University's Moorland-Spingarn Research Center*

This series of letters between Nicey Moore of Carthagene, Ohio, and Harvey, with whom she speaks of their impending wedding, were written in 1869 and 1870. In the letters, they coyly express their love for each other—how they stole each other's heart.

*September 14, 1869*

Dear Harvey,

I am well at present and hope these few lines may find you the same. There is something that compels me to write—yes something I have tried to keep which I cannot retain any longer that is love yes I love you. You have stolen my heart. Now I know that I have treated you wrong . . . I know that if you was to treat me now like I did you my heart would almost break. I would even receive letters from you and not answer them for a long time and some times not at all but I know that you are tender hearted and will forgive me for so doing.

      I am as ever
      Nicey

*October 26, 1869*

Dear Nicey,

Your kind and affectionate letter of September 14th was received with much pleasure was read and reviewed more than once. I hope you will not be mad at me for my neglect. Pardon me if it be an offense. I would not knowingly wound your heart. How could I think that one whom I so ardently love when I read poems with that ameliorating influence to my mind considering in you only. I cannot respond. I am not adequate to the task like two drops of water those sentiments run together. My heart has [been] stolen and I believe it's you that has it in possession. [W]ould you be willing to give me yours in return or would you refuse or persist in refusing to speak on this most solemn subject, subject of matrimony. I have no doubt you will censure me of forcing this question. I hope you will forgive me. You know I am weak minded and you say I am tender hearted but I don't think so. I [fault] my self for being hard hearted and always ready to return evil for evil but I need not inform you, you know [too] much about me already, although if

I had not such implicit confidence I could not
divulge the secret emotions of my heart with such
freedom. . . . I must bid you good night, happy
dreams attend you. . . .

And I will be your most
Devoted Harvey

## TO NICEY FROM HARVEY

*December 20, 1869*

Dear Nicey,

I don't know why I cannot cease to think of you,
and to love you, you say I have stolen your heart and
I can say this much you stole mine first and a fair
exchange is no robbery. . . . So I will present you my
heart and hand to accompany it provided you will
accept of them in return for the one that was stolen
from you. . . .

Good bye as ever,
Harvey

## To Nicey from Harvey

*June 18, 1869*

Dear Nicey,

I have read the contents of your welcome epistle
with unceasing pleasure . . .

That little sentence "what ever pleases you will
please me," would fill a volume, in detail—those
trusting endearing faithful words cling to my heart,
entwined there like the vine with its tendrils to the
verdant oak of the forest.

I hope you will never regret putting your trust
to my charge but there is one point I have ever
regretted since this subject has [been] agitated, that
is this, I regret that I am not prepared to treat you as
I would wish, my limited circumstances prevents
me from acting out my feelings to some extent . . .

I remain as ever,
H Moore

PS I have enclosed you an emblem as a token of
my love for thee, the ring which has no end, in
remembrance of me. Wear these if you will
accept . . .

## TO NICEY FROM HARVEY

*July 24, 1870*

Dear Nicey,

I have read and reread your kind and affectionate letter. The sentiments therein contained have lifted that [veil] that [seems] to encircle my heart . . . I will fear no more; as love to love meet with that agreeable affinity of purpose, and each mind is suited to its proper magnet, then do not say I have not confidence when I love you superior to all others and retain the strictest confidence in you as a lady. Those marks of true modesty and virtue and your good sense have [won] my heart. I so often am thinking of you . . .

Please say whether you will return the present or not, please say something. Now I must stop. [E]xcuse all blunders and mistakes and allow me to present my compliments as ever. Write soon

> PS My soul's place has become a person, through
> which the rays of those found eyes dart
> thrillingly,
> Then varied light, full as bed and radiant,
> Paints up the dark and chambers of my soul
> And this thou art to me a
> Brilliant vision

---

# Paul Laurence Dunbar
and Alice Ruth Moore,
1896–1898

*Schomburg Center for Research in Black Culture*

Paul Laurence Dunbar (1872–1906) was the most prominent African American literary figure of his time. Born in
Dayton, Ohio, to former slaves, Dunbar was taught to read
and write at an early age. He graduated from an otherwise
all-white high school in 1891, where he was president of the
school literary society, edited the school paper, and wrote
the graduation song. He published *Oak and Ivy,* his first
book of poetry, in 1892 at the age of twenty. Three years
later came *Major and Minors.* His early work represented
the first formal poetry to feature black dialect and drew fa-
vorable reviews in magazines such as *Harper's.* In 1896, at
the age of twenty-four, his reputation was firmly established when *Harper's* dedicated its entire review section to
him. By the time of his death in 1906, Dunbar was considered the poet laureate of black America, having published

twelve volumes of poems, five novels, and four volumes of short stories. He had also written two unpublished plays and scores of unpublished stories, poems, and lyrics. He also wrote the Tuskegee Institute school song at the request of Booker T. Washington and a campaign song for Theodore Roosevelt. One of these letters was written during his courtship of Alice Ruth Moore (1875–1935), a New York socialite, social activist, and writer, and the other after they were married. She was a founding member and officer of the National Association of Colored Women and worked on social causes with prominent women like Mary Church Terrell and Mrs. Booker T. Washington. She wrote and edited four books, including *Violets and Other Tales* (1895) and *The Goodness of St. Rocque and Other Stories* (1899), and contributed numerous articles and poems to magazines and newspapers like *Good Housekeeping,* the *Crisis,* and *McClure's.*

In one of the earliest letters from Dunbar to Moore, dated October 13, 1895, he wrote that he fell in love with her after seeing the picture that accompanied her article in the *Monthly Review.* "I know it seems foolish and you will laugh perhaps, or perhaps grow angry; but I can explain in one sentence. You were the sudden realization of an ideal. Isn't there some hope for me? I wish you could read my heart. I love you. I love you. You bring out all the best that is in me. You are an inspiration to me. I am better and purer for having touched hands with you over all these miles."

In another letter, written on October 28, 1895, he apologized for his outburst of emotion. "Dear Miss Moore," he wrote. "With saner thought, I have become convinced that my last letter to you proved me a most consummate donkey. I am sorry that I had no more sense than to take such an advantage of the consideration you have shown me.

"I feel sure that I have offended you and dread your answer. I know that my letter was rank, ill-considered and presumptuous, and I grieve that it should be so. For the feelings it expressed, I have no wish to apologize. I can't help them, am not ashamed of them and wouldn't change them if I could."

On February 5, 1897, Paul and Alice met—two years after beginning their correspondence. That evening, at a party in New York in Dunbar's honor, they were secretly engaged. The next day, Dunbar set sail for a six-month reading tour in Europe. They were married in New York on March 6, 1898.

Little Girl: Your letter has
these lines leave me heart-broken
I don't want to marry you
culture They are the easiest th
I want you for the qualities
you to possess. I will fur
firm, (if I can.) Darling,
future hold you. I feel th
to go thro' life at your side,
don't want to think of it.
say there is much you would
g yourself. Then, love, why d
have you not been a good girl?
life that you are ashamed
dear, I have been, he

## To Alice from Paul

*October 24, 1896*

Schomburg Center for Research in Black Culture

My Dear Little Girl:

Your letter has just been received and these lines
leave me heart broken. Darling, I love you. I don't
want to marry you for your brain and culture. They
are the easiest things in the world to find. I want
you for the qualities of heart which I know you to
possess. Darling, all of my dreams of the future
hold you. I feel that I could be happy to go through
life at your side, but without you, I don't want to
think of it. I want you to think of me darling as
your protector, even more than your lover. I know
that I wish to shield you from all the severities of
life and take you into the warm shelter of my heart
of heart.

## To Alice from Paul

*May 16, 1898*

My Dear Little Wife:

Here I am all safe and sound and would say happy if you were near me. Booker T. arrives tonight and speaks. I just got in some time to hear DuBois' paper. It was a fairly sophisticated article.

I am being and shall continue to be a good boy. It's a shame they want me to stay for the banquet . . . I am anxious to see little wife and to be home again in our own cozy nest . . .

# Meta Warrick Fuller

Meta Warrick Fuller (1877–1968) was an accomplished sculptor born to a middle-class Philadelphia family. She won a scholarship to what is now the Philadelphia College of Industrial Art and in 1899 went to Paris, where she studied with Auguste Rodin. She married Solomon Carter Fuller (1872–1953), a Liberian-born and American-educated neuropathologist and psychiatrist.

The letter that follows appears to be written by a heart-broken suitor who is contemplating their lives apart. It was written the year she left for Paris, where she remained for three years.

1157 S. 19th St.

June 189_

My dear Meta,

How
strange and yet natural
seems for me to sit
writing to you. Bu_
I'll try + be an
_imist + believe _hat
_ything is for the
_. I was glad, real_
_ to get your note
_nt to send you that
_ly written letter
_ France. That is
_ I was so anxious
_you about befor_
_the city for I
_ _p _ny _
_ _ _ _ Bu_

## TO META FROM SPENCER

*June 29, 1899*

My dear Meta,

. . . It's now evening and I am all alone in the house.
It is so pleasant and cool. The sun has set in a
cloudless sky. It is just such a sky as you and I used
to admire for it seemed to represent our lives so
truly; no cloud but just a halo of a great light which
we two foolishly took to be the rising sun. On it we
pinned all our future hopes and present happiness.
But too soon alas did it prove to be a setting sun.
Our hopes were blasted and we still are groping in
the darkness, waiting and waiting for the clear
light of day. What will it bring for you and me?
May it be to your comfort and may we both wander
through life looking back on our friendship not
mournfully, but pleasantly and may it prove a
balm. . . . I am afraid Meta in my anxiety and zest
I have overstepped my bounds, if so excuse me
and believe me,

> Your
> Tenuous friend
> Spencer

## PART TWO

# As the Century Turns

*T*HE HEADY OPTIMISM of African Americans during Reconstruction dissolved into despair as race riots and lynching threatened their security. Violence against African Americans was not limited to the South. In northern cities like Philadelphia and New York, African Americans were frequently attacked by whites and even forbidden from residing in some towns, like Syracuse, Ohio. Other municipalities, including Salem, Indiana, did not permit African Americans within its city limits. In August 1908, a riot in Springfield, Illinois, commanded national attention after white mobs set fire to black businesses and homes and killed innocent blacks. More than 5,000 militia were dispatched to the streets and more than 100 people were arrested.

With the start of World War I in 1917, about 350,000 African Americans served in the military and more than 600 were commissioned as officers. Many had hoped that as a result of their heroic patriotism African Americans would finally secure first-class citizenship, but many veterans returned to virulent racism and terrorism.

In 1918, eighty-three blacks were lynched, many of them while in military uniform. In what James Weldon Johnson called the Red Summer, more than twenty-five race riots swept through the country—mostly in urban areas as patriotic fervor following the war clashed with the heightened expectations of returning black veterans and festering urban problems brought on by the mass migration of blacks to the North. Thirty-eight people were killed and 537 injured in riots in Chicago that year, and more than 1,000 families, mostly African Americans, were left homeless due to property destruction.

The period following the war also saw the rise of black nationalism and Pan Africanism. In 1919, the first Pan-African Congress met in Paris with sixty delegates from the Caribbean, Africa, and the United States. One year later, Marcus Garvey drew 25,000 blacks to a rally at Madison Square Garden. But despite the harsh conditions for blacks during this turbulent period, African Americans continued to excel in many enterprises, and love prevailed.

# Mary Church Terrell
# and Robert Terrell

Mary Church Terrell (1863–1954), one of the leading women's rights advocates early in the twentieth century, was born in Memphis, Tennessee, to former slaves in the year of the Emancipation Proclamation. In 1884, she graduated from Oberlin College, where she was elected freshman class poet and editor of the *Oberlin Review*. Unlike many of her white female peers, Church graduated from the classical course, known as the "gentlemen's course," as it was considered too rigorous for women. The course of study was a year longer, required mastery of Greek, and ended with a diploma rather than a certificate.

Church, against the wishes of her father, entered the workforce as a teacher at Wilberforce University, upon graduating. Then, in 1887, she accepted a teaching position in Washington, D.C., at M Street High School. There she met Robert Terrell, the head of the Latin Department, whom she married in 1889. Terrell, a longtime resident of Washington, had graduated with honors from Harvard University the same year that Church graduated from

Oberlin. He went on to graduate from Howard University Law School and in 1901 became the first black judge in the country when he was appointed to the District of Columbia municipal court.

Meanwhile, Church had left her position as a teacher because married women were not allowed to teach. She instead committed herself to women's issues, associating with, among others, Susan B. Anthony. She then began to focus on black women's issues. She was appointed to the District of Columbia school board in 1895 and a year later became one of the charter members of the National Association of Colored Women. She traveled throughout the United States, campaigning for equal rights for women and African Americans, and served as a U.S. delegate to numerous international conferences.

The Terrells remained married until his death in 1925. In the letter that follows, she mentions their daughter Phyllis.

## To Robert from Mary

*Saturday, July 9, 1902*

My own Sweetheart:

I'm so blessed to own a man like you. As I was about to say—a knock, loud and imperative and shocking in its suddenness just made me jump out of my skin fairly and rush to the door. It was a special delivery from the one being in all this crowded universe from whom I should rather hear than from any of the other millions of its swarming human kind . . . If I had been at the coronation in the flesh today and had sat with the beautiful, sweet, womanly queen, I should have preferred to be with you and Phyllis, my dear. The more I roam the wide world over, the sweeter and more desirable my own home becomes to me. The more other people praise me and seem to appreciate my company, the more satisfying to my comfort and happiness are you and Phyllis. . . .

I could write all night. It's the only way I can be with you all night but as I am to leave here tomorrow morning, I suppose I should go to bed and get some rest. How much better I could rest with you tonight. . . .

Yours always Mallie

# Roscoe Conkling Bruce
# and Clara Burrill

*Howard University Moorland-Spingarn Research Center*

Roscoe Conkling Bruce, Sr. (1879–1950) was an educator and the son of Blanche Kelso Bruce, a former slave who served as a U.S. Senator from Mississippi from 1874 to 1880. The younger Bruce was named in honor of New York Senator Roscoe Conkling, a white man who led Senator Bruce to the front of the chamber when Bruce's fellow senator from Mississippi refused to escort him to be sworn in.

Roscoe Conkling Bruce served as Assistant Superintendent of the Washington, D.C., Public Schools. The letters that follow are between Bruce and Clara Burrill while she was a student at Radcliffe, and he was an administrator at Tuskegee Institute. In these letters, they lay out their wedding plans and the way they intend to conduct their lives as husband and wife. One striking aspect of these letters is Bruce's insistence that they function as equal partners, respecting each other as intellectual equals. They married in 1903 and had a son, Roscoe Conkling Bruce, Jr., who attended Harvard University where, in 1923, he was barred from the freshman dormitory because of his race.

*January 3, 1903*

My darling Wife—

... Dear heart, I have missed you a very great deal—how much no mortal but me can quite realize. (You, dearie, are an immortal!) I think of you literally all of the time. In my office my mind refuses to bind itself to routine duties and insists upon planning dresses and tomes and receptions and the Lord knows what for you. I love you, darling, with all my soul. My life you are. I pray that we may be always the creatures of poetry and romance that now we are; I pray that I may make you always happy; I pray that your life will not be narrowed by marriage but enlarged; I pray that we may be useful and worthy always. Let us, whatever comes, never forsake our scholarly interests; let us never degrade our ideals; let us always live on the summits of experience; and let us always be simple and noble and sensible and just.

I have been reading these last few days Cardinal Jerome's Idea of a University. His estimate of intellectual cultivation seems singularly first. Culture means enlargement of life; the scholar is the man of balance. But above intellectual cultivation Jerome would place noble feeling, pure aspiration. And more and more I am getting a similar point of view. Fine emotions give to life all its values; love gives even one a religion.

I hope you've written to Mama. The poor dear has written me a letter that would bring tears to your eyes. I love her, she loves you, and you must love her.

> Your devoted
> Ros

## To Clara from Roscoe

*January 31, 1903*

My darling—Just four months and four days from today you will be made, in accordance with the traditions of our civilization, my wedded wife; you are, thank Heaven, morally my Wife this moment . . . Come, dearie, tell me once for all that whatever comes you will marry me this June. Here I have made you a beautiful home, my salary will support you in comfort; my heart yearns for your presence; you have promised. Never, never harbor the thought, darling, that it is possible for June 4 to pass without our marriage. I love you devotedly. Ros

## TO CLARA FROM ROSCOE

*February 19*

My dear heart—

Yesterday and again today I was really disappointed in failing to hear from you. You, perhaps, don't realize that a letter from you is an event in my life. The nearer our wedding day approaches the more dependent am I upon you and your love. Darling, I hope and pray that I may prove worthy of your beautiful and absolute devotion. Your photograph smiles upon me this moment. Although you are probably in the midst of dreams, I can't help feeling that even the dreams are sometimes of your husband. He loves you with all his heart and soul; his life is consecrated to your happiness . . .

[E]very moment brings our supreme happiness a step closer. I sometimes watch the little hand on my watch as it spins around and around bringing you closer, closer, closer to my arms. I love you.

Devotedly,
Ros

## TO CLARA FROM ROSCOE

*March 12, 1903*

My darling—I got back from Mobile Tuesday and since my return have been as busy as a bee-hive! Roy Stokes arrived yesterday morning looking hale and hearty. He tells me, dearie, that you have been ill with la griffe. Why didn't you tell me, dear heart? I feel very bad, indeed, to know that, were you sick again, you would be tempted not to tell your Husband. Won't you promise to be a good girl and tell me if you ever get sick again? If you want to save me anxiety, you must tell me invariably when you get sick and just how sick you are. I'm glad that you are better now darling: please be careful to go about warmly dressed in heavy woolen underwear and your rubbers; be careful not to sit in a draft or in a cold room, etc., etc. I love you, Dimples, with all my heart and soul and it pains me deeply to learn that you have been sick—probably from avoidable exposure . . .

Give my love to all
Your devoted—Ros

## TO ROSCOE FROM CLARA

*Undated*

My own darling Ros:

You ask why in the "name o' common sense" I do
not write to you and sweetheart mine I have been
very unhappy lately because you write to me so
seldom.

I love you, darling, with all my heart and soul.
Your sweet letters bring me so much happiness.

I long to see you darling, I long to be held in your
arms and feel your sweet kisses on my lips.

Every day I count the days before our wedding.
I remember how happy I was when there were
"only" 150(!) days, and now there are less than 30.

Write to me soon and often dear.

My darling I love you, love you, love you,

Your
Clara

*May 1, 1903*

My darling—

One month more and I shall be with you in Washington; three days there after we shall be Mr. and Mrs. Bruce! Now, Dimples . . . we shall have from June 3 to June 17 for our honeymoon and we had, I think, best spend it quietly at Hampton. The Hampton Summer School doesn't open until much later and so, the winter school being closed, we shall be for all practical purposes alone. Moreover, I shall have a long wished opportunity to examine and study and perhaps tabulate some of Hampton's student biographies; this is very important for the success of our Bureau of Statistics here at Tuskegee. Mrs. Ferguson, a life-long friend of my family, has a home in Richmond and she hereby invites you and your husband to sail down the James to her home for three or four days. All this, with your permission, will be arranged. Of course on the fifteenth or the sixteenth we two will return from Hampton to Washington where I could make the address after which we'd leave for Tuskegee.

Dimples, there is a highly important matter that I must mention to you. Ask your woman doctor at

Radcliffe for literature on the physical aspect of marriage; I have already written to Doctor Francis for similar information. You see, dearie, we <u>must</u> know all about certain things; we must not in a matter of deep concern be ignorant blunderers. I know you don't like me to write these things to you but we mustn't be prudish. We must learn all we can. By the way, dearie, I really prefer that you shouldn't seriously attempt study after the fifteenth of May; now please don't. And, Dimples please tell me about the trouble. I am always careful to burn up any letter you wish me to.

The photographs of my dear little wife are beautiful. Have both of them finished up for me, darling. I want to place them here on my desk. . . .

With love for you all and above all for you—

    Your devoted
    Ros

P.S. I was delighted with your criticism of DuBois's book. You're a sensible child! I have bought the book and am contemplating a criticism of it for the <u>Atlantic</u>.

    R—

## To Roscoe from Clara

My darling:

The sweet letter that I received this morning from you I have read and re-read many times. It is perfectly true dearie, that if I were not so deeply in love with my sweet Husband I could do ever so much better work at Radcliffe. Often when I should be studying I am writing a letter to you or I am holding my book in my hand, looking at the printed page while my thoughts, my heart, are in Tuskegee with you. I often sit for hours dreaming of you. But, dearie, what can one expect of a girl whose soul is at Tuskegee and whose body alone is in Cambridge?

Dear heart, I love you with all the strength of my being. Every day I long more and more to see you to hear that voice I love so well, to look into your eyes, and to kiss your lips. This has been a bittersweet year, dearie. Bitter because we must be physically apart; sweet because we know that the love we bear each other rises above the physical separation and keeps us one tho' we are hundreds of miles apart. I love you, darling. . . .

Write to me soon, dearie. Dear heart, I love you with all my heart.

> Your
> Clara

*August 5*

My darling—

Just a note to tell you that I love you. How I long to see you tonight! Every moment in the day, dear, I think of my dear little Wife, and at night I dream of her. I certainly wish we were to be at Tuskegee together next year. My beautiful Wife would make life so sweet for me. Oh! How selfish I am.

Won't you come and kiss me; just once, darling?

Your devoted,
Ros

P.S. I find I've used eight sheets of paper and written visibly upon only two. I have written invisibly upon all the dear old story of my devotion.

R—

My darling,

So busy have I been during the last few days that I haven't had time to write to my darling but I have thought of him continually. Indeed, dearie, I have found difficulty in studying for my exams so wholly have all my thoughts been with you. You may be surprised to hear it, but I find more pleasure in thinking of you than I do in studying for mid-year exams . . .

Your letter with the quotation from Ed's came yesterday evening. Ed is very good to offer to help in our wedding expenses. We must have our wedding elegant, dearie, and yet as inexpensive as possible because we mustn't expect too much of Ed. Not any of us can boast of a super-abundance of this world's goods. . . .

Dearest, we are the ones who must largely decide whether our lives shall be happy or not, let us make them full of joy and gladness.

Oh dearie I shall be so happy when I am with you always. And, dearie, let's do all in our power to make others happy. Let us not be selfish in our love. Let us not leave our mothers alone and have them feel that in their last days they are unloved. Dearie neither you nor I have been as patient with them as we should have been—let's make amends. I want Mama to feel that as long as we have a home she has one too. I hope you'll let her know.

*Undated*

My darling Ros:

Every letter of yours I read a dozen or more times, and every night I sleep with your last letter under my pillow; not once have I gone to sleep at night since the 17<sup>th</sup> of Dec. without having the little crimson velvet box containing my beautiful ring under my pillow. I love my darling with all my heart and soul . . .

It is, dearie, as you say really divine that in less than 15 weeks we are to be Husband and Wife. Your last suggestion pleases me best—that we get married this very minute! I wish we could now say that we are to be married in less than 15 days—no, 15 hours . . .

Darling, your yearning to hold your bride in your arms and kiss her and kiss her is not more intense than her yearning to be held in her husband's arms and be kissed and kissed and kissed.

Dearie, as our wedding day approaches it seems that the beauty of our love become more apparent. It is a very pretty thing to see two young people marrying—each giving his or her life to the other, each living for the happiness of the other—the twain becoming one flesh. Darling, dearest, darling, I am eager for the three months to pass. I am eager for the time when we shall become Husband and Wife. I love you, dearie

Your own,
Clara

## To Clara from Roscoe

*Undated*

My dearest—In not writing to you these last two or three days I have treated you shamefully and I'm very sorry. The fact is, dear heart mine, that I haven't been able to call my time my own—(my own means yours). I've been pushed to get the material for the summer school prospectus into appropriate shape and I've been urged by the Executive Council to make a half-dozen committee reports now long overdue; and today I have just brought my work up to date. You will forgive me, I know, because you realize that my life is yours.

A dozen times today I have looked at the whisk broom and the ease your sweet hands embroidered for your Husband; and every time, my spirit kneels at your feet and do you homage and to express my heartfelt gratitude for all your loving kindness. How sweet of you to give your Husband the very first bit of embroidery you have made! He loves every stitch; he loves you. . . .

Your last letter I shall never, never forget. I treasure it and shall always.

Your devoted
Ros

*Undated*

My own Ros,

It is now one p.m. Sunday, and I do hope that one week from today you will be here with me. You have been away a long, long time, dearie, and I have learned, as Browning calls it, "The infinite pain of hearts that yearn."

. . . This morning I have seen several men walk down Parker St. who reminded me so much of you. How I should rejoice to see you coming down Parker St.

Oh my Roscoe, my Roscoe, how I miss you! It seems an age since last I saw you. Dearie I wish I could answer your entreaty, I wish I could be clasped in your arms and receive one little good night kiss.

There are not very many moments in the day when my thoughts are not with you. I lay awake at night and think of you. I do want you back dear. . . .

Your,
Clare

## To Clara from Roscoe

*April 14, 1903*

Today, dear heart, is the 14th of April. Isn't it splendid to realize that every minute, every hour, every day brings us nearer to the great event of our lives!

Your devoted,
Ros

## TO CLARA FROM ROSCOE

*Undated*

My dearest—I haven't heard from you for several
days. I expect you are very busy getting ready to
come to Cambridge. Well, I hope to meet you at the
train even though you come as late as the twenty-
ninth . . .

I am eager to get your views on a hundred
different things upon which I have rather loosely
thought. You and I have been apart so long that I
am a stranger to your views on many vital subjects
and you to mine. Temperamentally we are so much
alike. I flatter myself . . . that I fancy that our
reflective views don't fundamentally differ. My
religious views when you have them in all their
crudity, will seem at first very strange. I have no
cosmology worthy of the name. My sins of faith I
wrap in the insubstantial garments of agnosticism.
In my narrowed circle of faith I am an avowed
though not wholly consistent idealist. In idealism
you and I have already a common ground—a
ground that interchange of views and reflection
will indefinitely extend. To be sure we shall never
completely agree—no two critical thinkers ever did
or ever will or ever can. But our differences will be
differences of emphasis. Of sociology—my personal

religion!—we shall talk until you are weary. And you will teach me pedagogy—and many another thing besides. And in all things, dear, we shall understand each other and we shall sympathize and we shall help.

I can think of no happier career than a career in which you, as my wife, shall equally share. You have heard, I expect, how DuBois treats the poor uninstructed creature he has made his wife: the fault is not hers. But you and I shall be in ideal one. Before I go to Tuskegee I want you vitally to realize the significance of my—forgive me!—of our work there. Unless you are convinced through and through that Tuskegee is the place preeminent I should not greatly care to go there. But when you have thought the thing over and we have talked it over, I think you will agree with me. Don't think, dear, that I propose for you and Mother and me a life of isolation. Far from it. We shall travel abroad almost every summer; and even in the winter we shall go to various parts of this country on duty bound. But of this I shall talk later on.

Give my love to everybody.

In less than two weeks I shall once more fold in my arms the woman I love.

> Devotedly –
> Roscoe

P.S. Are you going to promise me to go regularly to the Gym while I'm in New York. I have a book on "The American Girl" that will convince you pretty thoroughly of the righteousness of my cause. And you'll simply have to obey—ahem!—me because New York is nearby and I shall be ready to enforce my orders at a moment's notice!

R—

# Nicey Moore and Jackson Okey

*Howard University's Moorland-Spingarn Research Center*

These letters, which span from 1905 to 1907, unveil the couple's plans to marry. Jackson attempts to assure his future bride that he would care for her sons as if they were his own.

*June 29, 1905*

Dear Loving Wife,

Yours of 26th [received] yesterday morning and found me enjoying the best of health. I was so very glad to hear from my loved darling one. Dear you cannot imagine how much pleasure and satisfaction it gives me to receive a letter and hear from you. My mind is now at perfect rest since you have promised to be my future companion, all that now bears upon my mind is the waiting for the time to come when we can be made one, though I consider that we are now one in heart, yet the blending words have not been said.

The first, or along the first days of October, I think will be a very suitable time for us to marry though it now seems to be a long way off but it will soon roll around. Dear love you are on my mind continually, often wondering what you are doing and wonder if you are thinking of me or not though I know you think of me for no one can love an other without thinking of them. I am so glad that the distance of miles can not separate one's love. Dear as I have been faithful in the past in writing to you so shall I be in the future. I shall write to you at least once a week and oftener if necessary, because I want to hear from you every week without fail, for I now look upon you, as no more, nor less, than my wife and esteem you as my wife in every particular and I accept your advice in any thing just the same as though we were actually married and reverence you as a wife of mine.

So dear pet, I leave the setting of the time and day of our marriage all to you and I will [acquiesce] in what ever you may do.

Dear you always told me that I needed a good wife and that you hoped that I would get a good woman for a wife, those words sunk deep in and took root in my heart, and more than that you have now decided to see to it that I have a good wife. I have no fears but that it will be so. I feel that it is the Lord's doings for He says that He will not forsake His little ones. Now dear as to Nellie visiting her aunt Adaline and Aunt Retta this summer a few days I leave that matter all in your hands. Do as you think best, as I expect for Nellie to be as much under your control as she is under mine, whatever you do on that line will be satisfactory to me, as your dear husband, I want her to help you do the work; and love, I want you to take all the rest you can for you are my wife and main dependence. So honey I shall always favor you all I can, for there is no one like you to me. Your consenting to be mine has given me more comfort and pleasure than every thing else since I have been in a lonely state.

Dear never fear, I am taking it just as quietly as I can these hot days, and I don't want you to work so hard all the time as you are doing. There is no need of it at all either. Ollie and Clyde send their regards to all and especially to Mamma with wishes that our union and life may be happy. . . .

Dear if I was by your side I could hug and kiss you until your lips would burn and say many things to you but I must stop.

With many kisses to you, Bye Bye dear.

I know you will write soon love.

> Your loving husband
> Jackson Okey

*July 6, 1905*

My very dearest loving wife:

Your very much esteemed letter of 3d was gladly received yesterday morning, which gave me much pleasure to read. This leaves me enjoying good health. I was glad indeed to hear from my loved one again and learn that you were well.

Dear I am resting entirely easy and comfortable on your promises, I certainly do confide in every word you say to me, doubting nothing. All that gives me any weary now is the long time of waiting for the day to come for us to become one.

October seems to be a long way off but it is the best we can do under the circumstances so with patience I will content myself the best I can and wait, (though it is trying).

Dearest love I am so accustomed to receiving your letters on Wednesday of each week, that I naturally look for a letter from you every Wednesday morning and I am just unnerved for a day or two before Wednesday comes, so you see what a plight I will be in should I fail to receive a sweet letter from your loving hand by Wednesday morning.

I hope you will not fail to start a letter to me

every Monday morning so I can get it by Wednesday and I will be sure to start you one every Thursday morning so you can get it by Saturday noon.

Dear don't fail to let me hear from you at least once every week until we see each other for you are resting on my heart all the time and ever will be. Say dear tell me, How are the boys taking our getting married now? They need have no fears; every thing will be all right. We will all get along all right.

... Dear I want you to ever remember that I am thinking of you all the time and don't forget me please.

My best love to you first with kisses, 1,000 and common love to Nellie and the boys in abundance. The children all join in love to you all ...

From the one who loves you tenderly and devotedly

Your loving husband,
Jackson Okey

## To Nicey from Jackson

*July 12, 1905*

My very dearest loving one. Your most welcome and sweet letter of 9th was duly received with pleasure this morning and found myself and all well as usual.

Dear love, I snatch time by the fore-top and hasten to reply, taking the advantage of the 13th unlucky day. We are having lots of rain and hot weather.

. . . Oct. 3d, the day which you have set will be looked upon by me to be a precious day, when you will be wholly mine and I will be yours to love and cherish. I will be on hands and at your service on that day if the Lord is willing.

. . . Dear I wish I could be with you this morning to talk with you and taste your honeyed lips. The days seem long and wearisome which I have to wait before I can see you. Yet I will run the race with patience remembering that the prize and crown will be worn at the end, no great things have ever been accomplished without work and patience. The fruits of our labor are always the sweetest.

Dear wife I feel more and more devoted to you the nearer the time comes for the blending of our love together. I know when we get married that it will be one of the hardest things in the world for me to stay away from you, because the very thought of your sweetness to me draws my heart and affections tighter and closer to you all the time when I think the time is so near at hand when I shall have a good true loving wife again. No other object or subject interests me as you do because you are mine in heart, and rest assured I am yours to all intents and purposes. Many kisses to you until we meet Oct. 3d. Love to Nellie and the boys. And Aunt E.B. Who will you want to marry us? Rev. Randall? I will expect a letter from you, my dear one next Wednesday. Your loving Husband

Jackson Okey

*August 17, 1905*

My dear loving darling:

Your very pleasant letter of 14th was duly received yesterday morning and as usual gave me much pleasure to read the contents written by your hand . . .

Dear I long so much to see you. I am thinking about you all the time. You are the first object on my mind every morning when I awake and the last at night, but dear honey the time is growing short until the 3d of Oct and I am simply longing for the time to arrive, for it seems that I can hardly wait, yet I am enduring it with all the patience I can.

My regards to Nellie and the boys after subtracting the largest portion for yourself.

The sweetest kiss for you.

Bye Bye Darling

Your sincere and devoted lover
Jackson Okey

## TO NICEY FROM JACKSON

*April 11, 1906*

My very dear loving wife:

. . . Dear you asked me so nicely to please send you $5.00. Dear I am glad that I am able to comply with your request. That is all right Dear love. I am truly yours and you are wholly mine and at any time that you need assistance from me just remember that you are only asking a devoted husband, and if it is in my power at all I will always be only too glad to do anything I can for my sweet darling one. Dear, enclosed I send you Post Office money order, calling for ten dollars. Dear I want to see you so badly I don't hardly know what to do. Dear I do love you with all my heart. I only wish I could be with you all the time if it was so I could. I would just show you how much I love you; because I cannot tell you on this small piece of paper . . .

> Love to Nellie and the boys
> A Kiss for you dear
> Your loving Dear
> Jackson Okey

# Emily Smith and
# Franklin B. Mallard

*Schomburg Center for Research in Black Culture*

The Smith family was a middle-class African American family in Savannah, Georgia. The letter, dated May 23, 1906, is to Charles Smith from a suitor of his daughter Emily. In the letter the suitor, Rev. Franklin B. Mallard, is seeking consent to marry Emily, a graduate of Talledega College.

409. Montgomery St,
Savannah, Georgia.

dear Mr. Smith :-

Possibly you
aware of the fact by this time
for your sweet little daughter
ith.
is the girl of my choice, and n
for her have lead me to ask
wife. This she has consented to.
should she become my w
suppose to make her ha
worldly happiness

## To Charles Smith from Franklin B. Mallard

*May 23, 1906*

My dear Mr. Smith:

Possibly you are fully aware of the fact by this time of my devotion to your sweet little daughter Emily R. Smith.

She is the girl of my choice, and my love and care for her have lead me to ask her to be my wife. This she has consented to.

I wish to say should she become my wife it shall be my one purpose to make her happy in this life so far as worldly happiness goes.

I am a poor man. One who has worked hard to acquire an education and I am one (if I do say it myself) who means to make my mark in the world, and take my place among the foremost men of my generation. My profession is not a money making scheme. But I have commenced upon my career with a salary of seven hundred and seventy dollars per year and of course that will be increased as the years come and go.

My church is not large as most congregational churches are not large. But I have the best people in Raleigh to work among. The field is promising and now is the time for us to start in and make a hit here in this needy field.

My church requests that I should marry as soon as possible. And you know how our people are about a single minister. One cannot make pastoral calls unless being exposed to criticisms.

With these facts before you I wish to ask you to give me your daughter Miss Emily R. Smith in marriage by Sept. 1, 1906 or not later than Oct. 1, 1906.

Anticipating your kindness in granting me this important request, I wish to offer many thanks and await your reply at your earliest possible convenience.

I am your sincere friend and brother,
Franklin B. Mallard

# James Weldon Johnson and Grace Nail Johnson

James Weldon Johnson (1871–1938) was a pivotal figure in the Harlem Renaissance and a seminal member of his generation. Perhaps known best for his critically acclaimed novel *The Autobiography of an Ex-Colored Man* and *God's Trombones,* a collection of poems, Johnson was also a lawyer, a field officer, and later a secretary of the NAACP. He also served as U.S. consul to Venezuela and Nicaragua.

In 1905, Johnson wrote "You're All Right Teddy," a campaign song for Theodore Roosevelt, and soon after was recruited to serve as a U.S. consul to Venezuela (1906–1908) and Nicaragua (1909–1912). He also wrote the lyrics to "Lift Every Voice and Sing," which became known as the Black National Anthem. Johnson also edited three important anthologies: *The Book of American Negro Poetry* (1922), *The Book of American Negro Spirituals* (1925), and *The Second Book of American Negro Spirituals* (1926). His *Black Manhattan* (1930) recorded the history of African Americans in New York.

Born in Jacksonville, Florida, Johnson was raised in a middle-class family. His mother was a schoolteacher and his father a headwaiter in a luxury hotel. Johnson attended Atlanta University, where he delivered the commencement address in 1894. Three years later, he passed the Florida bar examination. He moved to Manhattan, where he met his future wife, Grace Nail, who hailed from a family that had major real estate holdings in Harlem. They were married in 1910.

## TO GRACE FROM JAMES

*June 5, 1912*

My dear, dear Grace:

I have just returned from a five days trip in the interior and found that the ship from the south had arrived, but brought no letter from you. There was one from Mumsey and one from Dad, but none from you—and that made all the difference in the world. I can't tell you what a disappointment it was—This is the first time since I've been back that a ship has come in from the south and not brought me a letter from you. Please, sweetheart, make it a point not to miss another mail; we are getting only about two a month—and to miss a letter from you on one of them—I'm sure you understand what it means to me. I try to get a letter to you by every means possible, via Panama, or Guatemala, or Mexico.

. . . How are you, my little chicken? Are you contented and happy? I hope you are—No, it's strange—I want you to be contented and happy, and yet I should like to feel that you are not absolutely contented—you understand, do you not? And every day I'm torn by these same emotions, between my love for you that wants you always near me and my love that wants to spare you every pain. It was something of a struggle for me before I left New York; at times I felt that I couldn't bear to come back alone, that I would have to ask you to come with me, in spite of my determination—and then I felt that I couldn't bear to see you undergo again those long days of discontent and nights of unrest. The times I've seen the tears welling up in your eyes—and the worst of it all, it made me feel so clumsy, so helpless, the right word to say to you would not pass my lips and I sat like a dumb man; but it was not because I didn't suffer for you—Do you understand, sweetheart?

But as strong as the soul may be, the heart is oh, so weak, and my heart wants you, needs you. The rains have set in and the days are so dreary and the nights so lonely.

Well, three of the long months have passed, and it can't be much longer before we'll be together again. I am in hopes that next month will bring good news. There is generally a shift made in July, and I feel sure that we shall be among the fortunates. Don't get discouraged.

. . . I am plugging away at my literary work whenever I get a chance. I have a good idea for a new book. I received a nice, long letter from [illegible] on this last mail; he said our few songs were moving along fairly well and expressed the hope that I would bring up some new lyrics when I come . . .

Now, my best regards to Dad and Jack, a hug and a kiss for Mother, and for you, sweetheart, all of the deepest, purest and strongest love in my heart. A long, long kiss on the lips.

From your old James, who loves you very, very much.

James

My dearest "Son:"

How sweet of you to send such a long satisfying letter and the accompanying notes. I just reveled in reading them . . . , not once, but ever so many times, all to my heart's content. You poor "Son" "Mudder" does so miss you and is just counting the days that will mean your release from the tropics and permit us to truly live out an untiring honeymoon in some land [illegible] that will permit. You're right, absence does, like nothing else, I believe, afford an opportunity of testing one's self. Like you, I've had my test, if you must guess it's result; we shall even mean more to each other for this brief separation I'm sure. Just be careful to take care of yourself for me, as I'm for you . . .

You dear Son, you have a birthday, don't you on the 17th—I should love to send you something, but never mind, Mudder will have something here for you which won't get lost, so never mind, wait just a little longer;—I wish for you a realization of your desires, which will be the most acceptable and that you may live long! Just ever so long and that you may learn to love your Mudder more and more with each added year and that she may do likewise. . . .

Write soon and come home soon; just as soon as you can. . . . Love from all to you dear "Son"

Your devoted wife,
Grace

## TO GRACE FROM JAMES

*May 24*

My dear little old darling Mudder:

I've just received your letter of the 5th and the little note written two days later. The little love note with the pansy in it. Oh, you can never know how much I want you. The thought of you as far away from me makes me almost crazy, at times. But, never mind, little girl, it will work out all right. We are sure to win out, and it won't be so very long before we are together again, and on our way to a pleasant clime—Then, we'll have a real, sure enough, regular "Three Weeks" honeymoon all over. Do you want to?

. . . Oh, my dear, sweet little mudder, how I do miss you. The day is long and lonely without you—and the nights are so dreary—oh so dreary. I want my little mudder, and nothing but my little mudder.

A long, long kiss, my dear little wife and sweetheart.

Your old son,
J—

## To James from Grace

*January 13, 1914*

My dearest Son:

. . . People wear me out asking when you are expected back; one would think they had particular business with you; they kid me because when they ask:—"When have you heard from your husband?" I reply, that I hear each day. They think that next to impossible. Heaps and heaps and heapfuls of love for you; . . . Think of your "mudder" sometimes and come back to her just as soon as you can.

> Always devotedly,
> Your wife,
> Grace

# Isabella Vandervall Granger and William R. Granger, Jr.

*Schomburg Center for Research in Black Culture*

William R. R. Granger was a member of a prominent family of physicians in the early part of the twentieth century. Educated at Dartmouth College, Granger was the eldest brother of New York Urban League executive Lester Granger. Of the six male siblings, three were, like Granger, Jr., medical doctors, and two were dentists. Their father, William R. R. Granger, Sr., was also a physician. William Granger, Jr., married Dr. Isabella Vandervall, a gynecologist who had a practice in East Orange, New Jersey. These letters offer glimpses of the pain of separation endured by a two-career couple, and also speak to the contemporary dilemmas of a commuter marriage.

*February 20, 1917*

Mon Cher:

You must like to be scolded. Where is my to-days letter? Mean man to disappoint me. I lived the whole day only to answer the mailman's ring and get your letter. Then to be disappointed!

. . . I've had so many most unbearable disappointments lately that I feel another would be just about the last straw.

I won't promise to write you three times a week as you ask unless you promise never to disappoint me.

Is it a bargain?

## To William from Isabella

*June 14, 1917*

Dear Pau:—

I am waiting for you. Let me sit on your knee and
'splain away all the clouds which now envelope us.

Don't waste any more time. It's so short a time
before you leave me.

Waiting
Wife

*August 21, 1917*

Dear "Adam:"

It is not written in the Bible that Adam tempted Eve. I believe that it was the snake but in this case you are Adam and you are tempting Eve. How dare you hold before my eyes such a golden proposition as the one you made in your last letter? Suppose I were a rash Eve even as she of the Goddess of Eden was and accepted your proposition without thinking? What would happen then?

Your proposition sounded so glorious on first reading that I felt tempted to clap my hands in glee and telegraph you that I'd come right away; but soon the practical side of me began to work (it's too bad there always has to be a practical side) . . .

## To William from Isabella

*Sunday afternoon*

Another Sunday! And a beautiful day at that. The days go by all right enough till Sunday comes—but then oh what a hollowed mockery of former days! I don't even care to dress up. Last Sunday I dressed all up in my first pearls ever and earrings and tight white [jumper]. Then I complacently surveyed myself in the glass and practiced my nicest smile. The realization suddenly came over me that he would not come and admire me, that there wasn't the slightest possibility that my costume would be the least bit deranged from sitting on his knee . . .

# Mattie Hertzel Pearce and
# Edgar S. Henderson

The two letters between Mattie and Edgar are among 122 that were discovered in the trash bin outside 270 Convent Avenue, a building in Harlem where many prominent African Americans resided early in the twentieth century. Lana Turner, a resident of the building and, among other things, a Harlem bibliophile, said the letters were found in a battered black valise. The letters, which span from 1917 to 1922, document a passionate courtship that resulted in marriage, and offer a window onto a far more innocent age. In one letter, Edgar coyly remarks how their kissing episode "is about the best," but warns against such behavior in the future. "I want to impress on you the fact that you must not kiss other persons for in that way lives are broken. If you kiss that way at all kiss me as your future husband but I would rather you did not because though I have as a rule an iron hand on any feeling, there is no telling what might happen."

Mattie Hertzel "Hertzelie" Pearce was born May 25, 1897, in Bridgeton, New Jersey, and, upon graduating with a classical diploma, enrolled at the New Jersey State Normal School, from which she graduated in 1917. She taught at a segregated school in Carney's Point, New Jersey, until her appointment in 1920 as general secretary of the YWCA in Warren, Ohio.

It is likely that she met Edgar—who uses the name Ted—while attending the Normal School in Trenton, as he grew up in nearby Lambertville. Edgar graduated from Lincoln University in 1919 but in the interim, in 1918, was drafted into service. He moved to New York in 1919 and studied at Columbia University. The couple wed in January 1922, following a commuter romance. Soon after, Mattie gave birth to Carlotta. In June 1937, Hertzelie earned a Bachelor of Science degree from Columbia University.

## TO EDGAR FROM HERTZELIE

*January 14, 1919*

My dear friend, Mr. Henderson,

I received your letter and was very nearly overjoyed to hear from you. . . .

Well, Teddie, I've been itching to start this letter to you. I've just got to talk to you or go frantic. Why must I always be tormented with your hateful absence. When there is such an insatiable hunger for your beloved presence. Really, Ted, it's absolutely maddening to know that you are so near me and yet I see you so seldom.

If I had any control of my emotions I wouldn't love you when you're away, because it's almost cumbersome to have you occupying every cranny of my mind. In school, at home, abroad, always you; and I've found I can't work with you so prominent a part of my life and mind.

Ted, for Heaven's sake don't idealize me. I have not idealized you. Because in spite of my love (which is not the blind kind) I can see you with all of your faults. . . . You must love me because I'm so human, and weak and full of faults. That's the kind of love I entertain for you. Tis not the good or evil that I love, but natural human soul which represents an awful heartrending conflict of both.

Sometimes the evil predominates, and sometimes the good. It is an everlasting wrestling match for supremacy.

Goodnight, dear, and may I wish that your dreams come true.

Always, Hertzelie

## To Hertzelie from "Ted"

*April 23, 1919*

Dearest "baby":

How is my child feeling? By this time I hope she did not suffer any ill effects from last night because her "daddy" would feel very bad if she did. Ha! Ha! How do you like that form of salutation?

Oh dearie how I long to see you. My heart just craves for a sight of your dear face. It has been throbbing painfully all day it seems to me and I truly don't know what to do about it. If love is so painful why did it happen thus to me? . . . Why is it? I ask you to tell me, dear, you have been in love before and you know. Oh! Darling, you possess my heart forever and ever and it is up to you whether you will break it or not. Nevertheless whatever happens you and I shall love to all eternity. That piece called "At Dawning" seems to be ringing in my ears and expresses my whole feeling toward you, "I love you, I love you."

Nevertheless Hertzelie, though I write this above part of my letter to you yet it is only an introduction to far weightier things I have to say to you. I really do not know how to begin but I believe that kissing episode is about the best. You must know that there are certain limits persons have regarding their passions. I have a limit, you have a defined one too, but on my honor as a gentleman I would never have kissed you in that way if I thought that I was going too far. I never knew that you would lose control over yourself to such an extent as you did and it terrified me greatly. As I said before, such kisses are not allowed only with husband and wife and then only during a certain time when such become necessary. You know what I mean I hope without going any deeper. I must impress on you the fact that you must not kiss other persons for in that way lives are broken . . .

I hope you get well and that you love me more than ever as I do you. Concerning our marriage that is not so terribly far off and you said you would wait but if you get interested in another man (St. Thompson) I shall marry you immediately for I will not give you up to anybody else. . . . Oh! Why did you make me love you. I will say no more.

Ted

## PART THREE

# The Harlem Renaissance, the Depression, and a New Deal

THE GREAT MIGRATION saw some 500,000 blacks leave the South between 1923 and 1924 and fueled the Harlem Renaissance (1919–1934), a period of prolific achievement by a group of young African American poets, writers, and artists.

Among the stars of this movement were many of the writers and artists whose letters follow. Included are the letters of Countee Cullen, who in 1925, at the age of twenty-two, published *Color,* his first volume of poems. The letters in this volume were penned to Cullen by Yolande DuBois, the daughter of W. E. B. DuBois, who was briefly married to Cullen.

Also included here is a letter to A'Lelia Walker, the daughter of Madam C. J. Walker and the grand hostess of many parties that brought together Harlem Renaissance luminaries. And the correspondence of glamorous film star Fredi Washington (who starred in the classic *Imitation of Life*) to her husband reveals her playful side.

# Countee Cullen and
# Yolande DuBois

*Yale University Beinecke Rare Books and Manuscript Library*

Countee Cullen (1903–1946) was an influential figure in the Harlem Renaissance known best for his volume of poems *Color* (1925), which stoked the flames of the literary movement. Perhaps his most famous poem is "Yet Do I Marvel," in which he speaks of African American alienation. "Yet do I marvel at this curious thing: / To make a poet black, and bid him sing!" His poem "From the Dark Tower" gave A'Lelia Walker's parlor its name, "Dark Tower." Born in New York City in 1903, Cullen graduated Phi Beta Kappa from New York University and received an M.A. in English from Harvard. He began to write at the age of fourteen, and by twenty-two, during his senior year in college, had already published *Color*. His work was widely published in magazines such as *Harper's* and *The Nation,* and he was one of the first African Americans to receive a Guggenheim Fellowship. His collection of poetry *On These I Stand* was published posthumously in 1947.

The letters that follow were written by Yolande DuBois, a college sweetheart and daughter of W. E. B. DuBois, the leading intellectual of his day and editor of *The Crisis*. The letters begin while Cullen was a student at New York University and DuBois attended Fisk University. The couple was married for a brief period.

## To Countee from Yolande

*January 24, 1924*

*(Fisk University)*

Countee dear,

Probably you have noticed my capacity for turning up, just as you've crossed me off your list of acquaintances. I ought to be studying this minute but I'm afraid if I wait much longer you'll never speak to me again and that would be tragic. . . .

I think about you many times during the day and look forward to my return when I hope you will come over as you used to and read your poetry to me. It would be a relief even to fuss with you just now. Just the other day I thought of you so much; why? Well, your song—"I've something sweet to tell you;" kept ringing in my ears. I could shut my eyes and see once more the sand, the sea and sky, and your eyes—so tender, so earnest and so young. You see, in spite of my silence I don't forget.

Good night my dear.

Love,
Yolande

## TO COUNTEE FROM YOLANDE

*August 12*

My dearest—

Your letter from Alexandria came at quite a psychological moment. I was feeling as blue as indigo and lonely. I also felt that there was something strange about being so far from you. I tried to behave and have faith in your love—the fact that you'd come back to me. Do you remember telling me that we'd find a sun-lit pathway through the thicket? I've read that letter over and over to help me through the long days of your absence.

. . . Just when do you land in New York? I suppose I will have gone but I'll come back unless you can come down. I do so want to see you. By now you must be convinced that there is still a very strong echo in my heart. Come back and really kiss my finger. It's lonely for you.

As you have judged, I'm going back to Baltimore. I received a permanent appointment just lately and mother thinks I'd better teach there at least a year longer. I will be very far away and I come home quite often. Even so I hate to leave you in New York. I'm very jealous you know . . .

I wish you were here to dance with me—I have always loved to dance with you . . .

Remember dear—I'm waiting—come back to me—soon, please. I love you.

Always yours,
Yolande

Countee—

Your special came Monday night. Hard and unkind as it seemed to me—I thank you for it. That which I deserve I have no right to complain of.

However unpardonable my faults may be— my [illegible] has been in being too stubborn and bad-tempered and in saying foolish smart things which I didn't mean—and never will mean. And yet beneath my stubbornness I have loved you faithfully . . . and always will. I love you with all my heart and soul. I pray that someday you will come to believe in me again. There can never be anyone else. Down the years you will find me waiting.

I want to see you—I am coming home mainly for that, secondly to see the doctor! Won't you meet me? If I told you I was ill and really wanted to be with you, you would conclude, as you did about the telegram—that it is a fictitious illness. I admit that I do very much want you to come. Won't you please? Now whether you believe it or not—I am feeling very badly this day—physically I mean. My mental discomfort is understood.

I am leaving Baltimore on the "Montrealer"—leaving here at 3:25—reaching the Penn Station at 7:45 p.m.—I suppose all times are standard now.

Always,
Yolande

# Robert and Hattie Haynes

These letters are in the possession of renowned Los Angeles-based artist Betye Saar and were written to her Aunt Hattie, who eventually married her suitor, Robert. Saar used some of the letters exchanged between the couple in a series of works in which she sewed them together, painted them, and then collaged them to a canvas background.

*April 15, 1928*

Hattie! Dearest One,

With pleasure untold I write you. This beautiful,
beautiful lonesome afternoon. I'm thinking of you all
the while. The thought of you is all pleasure to me. In
space we are quite some distance apart, but in Heart,
we are near. In leaving you at night the time it takes
me to get home is so short I cannot realize it. Why!
Because I am thinking of you every bit of time I'm
running. Talking to myself to you. Oh! But you
cannot imagine how happy you have made me. It
worries me when I hear you say "Oh! I was a little
blue today." I don't see how you can become <u>Blue</u> if
you think of me the way I think of you. Of course my
thoughts are so much of the future, as well as the
present. You may be looking at the future with such
doubt that it brings on "The Blues." Look forward for
Light and you will get it for there is no Darkness
where there is Light. I Love You. Now if you can say
the same, and and be not from the Lips, but The
Heart, then there will be Light. When there is Light
there be Happiness. Sorrow and Happiness can not
dwell together. I am asking you to Trust in, and
Believe Me.

"I Will Not Deceive You."

. . . You have so many sweet ways I adore. You have come nearer the expectations of what I've longed for in Woman. I like your looks. I like your ways. I like your ideas. I like you for My Self. And I could Like You Always. . . .

I will now prepare for bed, hoping to have sweet dreams of you . . .

Love and Sweet kisses from yours . . .

Bob

## TO HATTIE FROM BOB

*June 18, 1929*

Hattie! My Dearest One,

A word or two to you to say I'm thinking of you though I be absent. . . . Have been thinking of you all day. Thinking how sweet you are to me. How can I but love you. Yes! Love you is no word to describe it. This will be for you on your return for Thursday morning. . . . I'm so lonely tonight waiting to see you for this is our night . . . I can say truthfully I have no worries and that is a lot to say. You have made my life a real one of Happiness and I Love You. The Love I have for you I've never had for any one before. I never feel as if I want to cheat on you. I have been a cheater in my time, but I have no desire to cheat on you. It seems as if I'm come to the end of the road. I'm Satisfied and contented. My only and longing desire is to make you Happy. Make you as you have made me. You need never worry about me in our absence for certainly all will be good. Closing I'll say good by and may God bless you. I remain as ever yours in love.

"Daddy"

# A'Lelia Walker and
# Dr. J. Arthur Kennedy

*A'Lelia Bundles Collection*

A'Lelia Walker was the daughter and heir to the fortune left by Madame C. J. Walker, the self-made millionaire who invented and manufactured hair products for black women. Madame C. J. Walker died in 1919, leaving her fortune and business to A'Lelia. During the Harlem Renaissance,

A'Lelia operated a literary salon from her townhouse at 108 West 136th Street. The "Dark Tower," as it was called, provided a place for young artists and writers—among them Langston Hughes, James Weldon Johnson, and Countee Cullen—to discuss their work.

A'Lelia married J. Arthur Kennedy, a physician and surgeon in Chicago, in 1926. He was her third husband. This letter was written while Walker was on an extended trip to Europe, Africa, and the Middle East.

## To A'Lelia from Dr. J. Arthur Kennedy

*December 8, 1921*

My Dear Darling Lelia:

. . . Oh, how all other times seems to drag at this slowest pace since your departure. I think of the whole of Europe in terms of you and I am praying and praying each day for your safety and pleasure; that your entire tour may be like . . . a beautiful long road strewn with fragrant crimson flowers; it's end of which terminates within the circumference of my arms.

I do hope that you are well and happy and shall remain in that ecstatic state every moment of your life. I am planning now to increase that state of happiness for my darling and make it permanent, while on this earth. . . .

I presume everybody is looking forward to the wonderful Xmas tide, which is soon to flow in upon us, however I am not included with its number who are expecting wonderful pleasure and etc. because you, dear Heart, constitute my entire life and pleasure, Xmas included and of which I am now deprived, eliminates all ecstasies or even the elements which enter unto the compound. Yet I shall exist until you return to me at which time my happiness will break the flood gates of melancholy and flow out into that beautiful field of life, turning with the golden sunshine of success and with it beautiful crimson flagrant flowers of achievement and ultimate victory.

Sincerely,
Jack

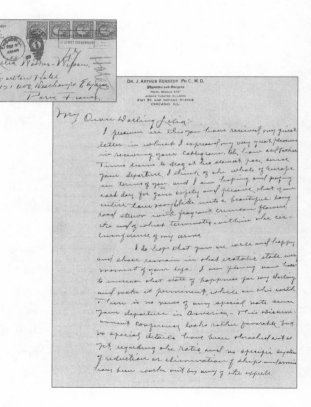

# Henry Arthur Callis
# and Myra Colson

*Moorland-Spingarn Research Center*

Henry Callis (1887–1974) was a medical doctor and academic affiliated with Tuskegee Institute's U.S. Veterans Hospital and Howard University's School of Medicine, where he was a founding member of the national fraternity Alpha Phi Alpha. Myra Colson (1892–1979) was a social worker, social science researcher, and YWCA administrator. Her father, James M. Colson, was principal at Virginia Normal and Collegiate Institute, and her mother and siblings were also educators. The letters in this collection trace their torrid courtship between 1925 and 1926. Myra and Henry did eventually marry and remained devoted to each other until his death in 1974.

## To Myra from Arthur

*December 29, 1925*

My Myra, My Myra:

My spirit is overwhelmed at the good things which came to me yesterday. Your letter reached me as a fitting conclusion to an eventful day . . . At eleven o'clock I entered the "Y" building to find your letter awaiting me. I had been seeking it surreptitiously all day long. I had despaired of receiving it, but wanted to go to my room alone to write you before I lay down to sleep for the night.

When I reached the room I found pleasure in the mere possession of your letter. Finally I sat down to read it. Its extravagance filled me with awe rather than egotism. I knew you would miss me a great deal. I did not dream the effect of our separation would be so great. When I reached the ending I was overwhelmed completely. Emotions overcame me. I slipped from the chair to my knees, half kneeling, half lying across my bed. I could not write so I went to bed. My sleep was restless. I awakened continually to reach for your letter, to make sure I had read and was not dreaming . . .

. . . For so long it has occurred to me that we have "belonged" to each other. Still I have endeavored to eschew my "possession behavior." I believed that some day you would give yourself, or rather find out that neither of us is any longer complete without the other. Completeness rather than possession is more truly expressed by the "my" and "your" which comes to be used between us. So do we miss each other. So do we long for each other. So do we reach out across the spaces and come to each other a thousand times a day. . . . I am happy that I love you and possess your love and that I bring to you, also, the honors which have been heaped upon me.

Your Arthur

*January 7, 1926*

Myra dear:

The love of you, the longing for you makes me physically ill. I am unfit to attempt anything. Such absolute weakness seems incredible. Situations that require the utmost marshalling of reserve to approach, under other circumstances would be as nothing. In your absence I have found the keystone of my being. The center at once of my strength and my weakness.

I should be away from this spot. I am going. But how much easier it would be to sit here in silence with my eyes invited on space. Myra, I am miserable without you, dear.

With love,
Arthur

## To Myra from Arthur

*January 18, 1926*

Dear Myra:

Your letter was such a happy message today. I expected it and yet I tried to keep my anticipation subdued sufficiently so that I should not be disappointed had it not arrived. As I read the reluctant messages of your spirit, I could have drawn you to me and hold you in such close embrace. It does seem that all the rest of the world is inconsequential. By that token each of us must be under the spell of the Eternal Principle completely. As for me, I have been of little value without you for these past weeks.

This is the last letter until your returning! It seems so good, too good to be other than a dream. So long have I awaited this night. Yet three, maybe four, days and nights stretch between us. How quickly I want them to fly, yet how difficult it will be to claim impatience unrelieved by the pen. So hurry, Myra.

My head is in a whirl with little plans for your welcoming. I scarcely know what I'll do, or what I want to do. I just want to make you glad to get

back. I hope I shall not be too excited or idiotic . . .
All is being made ready for you and the entire
apartment shall be yours to roam around in as you
please. All I ask is to sit by and watch you . . .

>With all my love dear,
>Arthur

*January 17, 1926*

My Myra:

I have missed you so very much today, dear. Perhaps it has been because I have realized so keenly how near at hand your arrival is. It has been so good to know that next Sunday I should be near you. The increased lonesomeness has been tempered with the joy of anticipation. I scarcely know how I shall contain myself for the next few days. . . .

How I welcome sleep. It will make so many of the hours pass quickly, dear.

> With love,
> Arthur

## TO ARTHUR FROM MYRA

*Tuesday (undated)*

My sweetheart,

The happiest moment since you left was the one
when I returned home alone an hour ago and found
your telegram. I had waited and waited for it since
midnight and when I imagined for it at the office
and did not find it was heartsick . . . I had it on the
table before me as I at[e] my dinner. It means more
than any piece of paper I ever had. . . . I think I
should feel better now that I have had some word
from you . . . But any doubts I had are quite swept
away by the revelation you going has meant. I
cannot think of my life except with you as an
intimate pair . . .

I returned home yesterday about 4:30. You
cannot imagine how I felt when I came in and
found all your things gone. . . .

I meant everything I told you before you left. I
am completely yours. Whenever you need me I am
ready to come. . . .

Love, Myra

# Fredericka (Fredi) Washington
## and Lawrence Brown

*Schomberg Center for Research in Black Culture*

Fredi Washington (1903–1994) was born in Savannah, Georgia, where she was the third of nine children. She went to New York in 1919 at the age of sixteen and began her career as a chorus girl at the Alabama Club. She was later featured in the landmark *Shuffle Along* and in 1926 appeared in *Black Boy* starring Paul Robeson. She sailed to Europe with Al Moiret as part of a dance act called "Fredi and Moiret" and upon her return to the United States in 1928 launched her film career. In 1930, she appeared with Duke Ellington in the short feature *Black and Tan Fantasy,* which in all likelihood is how she met Lawrence Brown, a trombonist in Ellington's orchestra. Three years later she starred with Robeson in *Emperor Jones,* followed in 1933 by *Drums in the Night.* During this period she also had lead roles in three plays: *Sweet Chariot* (1930), *Singing the Blues* (1931), and *Run Lil' Chillun* (1933).

In July 1933, Washington married Lawrence Brown, which was widely reported in the press. While at the time she announced that she would retire from show business, a year later she earned national acclaim for her role in *Imitation of Life,* and she later costarred with Bill Robinson in *One Mile from Heaven* (1937). She also appeared with Ethel Waters in the play *Mamba's Daughter* in 1939 and had a lead role in the all-black production of *Lysistrata* on Broadway in 1946.

Washington was politically active and participated in the boycott campaigns and picket lines organized to integrate businesses along 125th Street. The campaigns were organized by her brother-in-law, the Rev. Adam Clayton Powell, Jr., the renowned congressman and pastor of Harlem's Abyssinian Baptist Church. Powell was married to Washington's sister, Isabel. Washington was also cofounder and later executive director of the Negro Actors Guild.

## TO LAWRENCE FROM FREDI

*December 13, 1933*

Darling—

First of all let me remind you that we're married
eighteen weeks today. And I am so utterly happy.
So happy that it's impossible to explain to you. It's
something that can be told only with the eyes and
right now, I can't see you.

So far today, I haven't had a letter. I hope one
comes before the day is over. Didn't you write to
your baby?

. . . Be sweet darling. It won't be long now.

I love you, I love you, I love you my own darling.

Your Baby dear

Hello Sweets,

Theey're having a little party here tonight and they're playing soft love music and singing and do I wish you were here with me. Just the sort of music I'd like to dance to with you. Would you hold me close? Be sweet my darling.

Love, Fredi

POST CARD

1979 N

Mr. Laurence Brown
c/o Duke Ellington's Orchestra
R. K. O. Palace Theatre
Chicago, Ill.

A LOVE NO LESS

## POSTCARD FROM FREDI TO LAWRENCE

*Care of Duke Ellington Orchestra,*
*RKO Palace Theatre, Chicago, Ill.*
*Postmarked June 22, 1932 — Winston-Salem*

Hello Sweets,

They're having a little party here tonight and they're playing soft love music and singing and so I wish you were here with me. Just the sort of music I like to dance to with you. Would you hold me close? Be sweet my darling.

Love,
Fredi

EASTER GREETINGS TO THE SWEETEST LIL
EASTER BUNNY I KNOW.

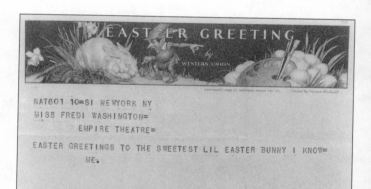

NAT801 10=SI NEWYORK NY
MISS FREDI WASHINGTON=
        EMPIRE THEATRE=
EASTER GREETINGS TO THE SWEETEST LIL EASTER BUNNY I KNOW=
        ME.

## TELEGRAM FROM FREDI TO LAWRENCE

*Care of Duke Ellington*
*Ritz Carlton*
*August 9, 1939*

THANKS FOR SIX OF THE HAPPIEST YEARS I
HAVE EVERY [sic] KNOWN. MAY EACH OF THE
COMING YEARS CROWN OUR LIVES WITH EVEN
MORE HAPPINESS AND UNDERSTANDING,
FLOWERS, BEAUTIFUL LOVE.

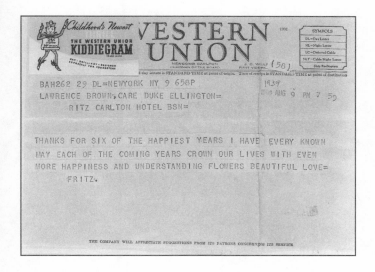

# Charles Drew and
## Lenore Robbins

Charles Drew, a surgeon, educator, and researcher is widely credited for his work in the field of blood plasma that saved millions of lives. In 1942, he became director of the Red Cross's drive to collect and store blood. Drew founded two of the world's largest blood banks, and his research on the storage and shipment of blood plasma prevented millions of deaths. A surgeon at Howard University Medical Center, Drew was the first African American to serve as an examiner on the national medical examination board.

Born in Washington, D.C., Drew attended Amherst College on an athletics scholarship. He was the captain of his track team and a star halfback on the football team. Two years after graduating from Amherst, he attended McGill University Medical School in Montreal, where he began his research on blood groupings. In 1933, he returned to Washington, D.C., to teach pathology at Howard University.

In 1940, while earning his Doctor of Science degree at Columbia University, he wrote a dissertation on banked blood that resulted in the British government calling on

133

him to set up England's first blood bank. His success there led to the Red Cross recruiting him to establish a blood bank program in the United States. He created the refrigerated bloodmobiles that are still used by the Red Cross today. He resigned from the Red Cross in protest after the U.S. War Department ordered the segregation of blood by race. The practice continued until 1949. He received many honors, including election to the International College of Surgeons, and the NAACP's Spingarn Medal.

In 1939, Drew married Lenore Robbins, whom he had begun courting while she attended Spelman College in Atlanta. In 1950, he was killed in a car accident while driving to a conference at Tuskegee.

## To Lenore from Charles

*Western Union Telegram sent to Spelman College*
*Date unclear*

STILL IN A DREAM I WALK LIKE ONE
ENTRANCED AND THINK OF YOU =

CHARLIE

## To Lenore from Charles

*April 9, 1939*
*Washington, D.C.*
*Easter Sunday at twilight*

Lenore,

With a heart that's full with a new found joy my
thoughts turn to you as the day closes and a sigh
rises as an evening prayer to ask whatever gods
there be to keep you safe for me. Since first meeting
you I have moved through the days as one in a
dream, lost in revery, awed by the speed with which
the moving finger of fate has pointed out the way
I should go. As the miles of country side sped by on
our return trip I sat silent and pondered on the
power that lies in a smile to change the course of a
life; the magic in the tilt of a head, the beauty of
your carriage and the gentleness that struck so
deeply.

Later when I become more coherent I shall say
perhaps many things but tonight this one thing
alone seems to ring clearly. I love you.

Charles

## To Lenore from Charles

*April 16, 1939*

My Sweet,

Man at his best is an odd creature and I as the least of men am the oddest of creatures at best, but never have I, even at my worst, acted as strange as I have for the past week. For years I have done little but work, plan and dream of making myself a good doctor, an able surgeon and in my wildest moments perhaps also playing some part in establishing a real school-of-thought among Negro physicians and guiding some of the younger fellows to levels of accomplishment not yet attained by any of us. I have known the cost of such desires and have been quite willing to do without many of the things that one usually regards as but natural. Then I met you and for the first time mistress medicine met her match and went down almost without a fight. Life suddenly widened its horizons and took on new meaning. I knew clearly just how lonely I had become, just how badly I needed someone rather than just something to cling to, someone to work for, rather than just a goal to aim at, someone to dream with, cherish from day to day, and share the little things with, the smiles and if need be the tears that will sometimes come. When I first kissed your hand it was almost reverently clear for even then I felt an inward surge that was inexplicable. When you walked I felt lifted by the graciousness of your carriage; when you talked it was your gentleness that struck so deeply; when you smiled there was sweetness that only a fortunate few can carry even from an unspoiled childhood to full glorious womanhood; poised but vibrant, there was something which responded in me and left a glow which still suffuses my whole being and warms my heart. It's a grand feeling Lenore. The only rash, unplanned, unpremeditated thing I've done for years is already paying dividends in a thousand delightful ways.

Like Elizabeth Browning I feel that a new source of strength has come to me, and I am grateful.

"How do I love thee? Let me count the ways. I
    love thee to the depth and breadth and height
My soul can reach when feeling out of sight
For the ends of being and ideal grace.
I love thee to the level of every days'
Most quiet need, by sun and candlelight.
I love thee with the breath, smiles, tears
Of all my life"

    And so
    My love
    Goodnight,
    Charlie

## TO LENORE FROM CHARLES

*April 21, 1939*

Lenore,

On my mother's birthday you wrote me the loveliest letter I've ever received, the kind I've always wanted from someone like you. It is symbolic for me, joining you in my mind and heart, you about whom all my future revolves, to all that is finest, dearest, loveliest in the years that have passed, that part which has clung to at least a few ideals, has striven to be decent and achieve simply because it would please one of earth's sweetest souls, my mother. I should like to do things that make you proud, seek you out when I'm tired, tell you my stories of the days' work, the things I dream about. Three things there are which are necessary for happiness—someone to love, to be loved by some one, and a job to do. You can teach me to be those things which you'd have me be and my joy shall be in learning. What would you have me be? What are things I can do that will make you most happy? It seems so strange that having been with you so little I could miss you so much, that days which are so terribly full could have so much of emptiness in them, that nights which should be spent in sleeping are wide eyed with a lingering loneliness.

I'm jittery with anticipation, impatient that I can't get things going faster, that I can't find out first what plans have [been] laid out for me so that I may know what to tell you. Most of my bridges to the past have been destroyed without regret. The future seems to glow in the radiance of you. Lenore have you ever looked for anything for a long, long time and then suddenly found it, and knew at once you had. Its indescribably grand. It changes one, changes the world and all that's in it, adds meaning, purpose and a new succession of goals. Up to now I have gone alone. I never want to again. Just thinking of you has helped so much, loving you means so much more.

Your last letter leaves me with almost a feeling of pure gratitude. It gave me a peep into your heart. You darling, I do thank you.

Charlie

## To Lenore from Charles

*June 9, 1939*

My Wife,

I love you, I miss you, I want you; the whole place is empty without you.

Charlie

## PART FOUR

# World War II

$\mathcal{M}$ORE THAN three million African Americans registered for service in the Armed Forces under the Selective Service Act of 1940. By 1944, when the Army was at its peak, more than 701,678 African Americans served in the Army; 165,000 in the Navy; 17,000 in the Marine Corps; and 5,000 in the Coast Guard.

Following the attack on Pearl Harbor, the United States Army opened a school for black pilots at Tuskegee, the first such training school for African Americans. An estimated 600 African American pilots received their wings during World War II, with the Tuskegee Airmen distinguishing themselves for their heroism. By the end of the war, more than one million African Americans had performed active duty, including Sgt. William Scott III and Private Lee Turner, whose love letters are included here. Also included is a telegram sent in 1943 to Flournoy Miller, an actor, comedian, and producer, from his wife Bessie.

The dearth of contemporary letters, particularly of the

quality so common up to the 1940s, is also due to the growing popularity of greeting cards, which convey nearly every emotion, and improvements in technology that resulted in the proliferation of telephones in households after World War II, and the understandable wish for privacy by people who are still alive and unwilling to expose their most intimate world.

# Sgt. William Alexander Scott III
# and Marian Willis Scott

William Scott served in an all-black unit that in 1945 helped to liberate the Nazi concentration camp at Buchenwald. While in the Army, between 1943 and 1946, he frequently corresponded with his high school sweetheart Marian, whom he married while on leave in 1944. Marian, whom he nicknamed Susie, graduated from Spelman College in 1945. The letter that follows was written a month before they were wed.

A LOVE NO LESS

*July 29, 1944*

Dearest Darling,

I wish so much you were here with me. I went out to D.B.'s this evening and had a very nice time. They had all heard about my engagement and wanted to see my ring. They thought it was very pretty. Darl I'm crazy about it too. I sure hope I get a letter from you Monday and I hope with all my heart you can come home soon. Scottie I love you with all of me. . . .

I'm laying here looking at your picture and just wishing with all my heart you could step out and be here with me. I had the best ole dream about you last night. I can hardly wait to go to sleep so I can be with you again.

Darl can't you work out some way for us to be together soon? I suppose the question is out of your power huh? But Darl I do wish we could be together. I wish you'd come here and when you had to leave I could go on back with you and stay awhile. Darl, if we were married couldn't we be together more often? Don't you want to be with me huh Scotties?

> I'm all yours.
> Susie

# Lee and Ida Turner

*Lana Turner Collection*

Lee Turner was born in 1909 in Swainsboro, Georgia, where he was raised by his grandparents. Upon graduating from Fort Valley Normal and Industrial, he went to West Palm Beach to find work. There, in 1941, he met Ida, but a year later he was drafted into the service. While he was on furlough from the Army in August of 1943, he and Ida were married. In 1945 he was discharged from the Army, and five years later they had the first of six children. The letters that follow were written while he was in the Army.

A LOVE NO LESS

## TO IDA FROM LEE

*Undated*

My darling wife,

Just a few lines to let you know that I am well and thinking of you. I hope you are well and doing fine.

Well darling I just came from the movie. It is 10:30 so our lights are out and I am writing this in the bathroom. I am so worried I just had to write you. Look like nothing I do will ease my mind. I believe if I had to go like this much longer I'll be crazy. My mind is on nothing but you. I thought we would have been gone from here by now, but we are still here, but still looking to leave any time. If I only knew where we are going when we do leave. I hope we move somewhere near. Darling I am so lonesome for you I don't know what to do. It hasn't been two months since I saw you but it seems like it has been two years. Darling I miss you so much. If I did not love you it would not matter but I do love you dear and always will. You are the only one I'll ever love dear. I wish I was there now so I could prove it and to share our little home with you; but since it so I can't be there all I can do is think of it. Darling I hope you are thinking of me the same way. I'll be glad when this is over so we can share each other's lives and live lovely together until death parts us. Darling that is the only thing that will part us when we get together again. . . .

Well darling, you must take good care of yourself and be sweet and true for me, and love me as I do you.

Give my best regards to all and write me real soon. Darling I love to read letters from you.

> Your true loving husband
> PFC Lee A. Turner

I love you so much dear. Do you still love me?

## To Ida from Lee

*Undated*

My darling wife,

Just a few lines to let you hear from me . . . I wish I was with you right now, but since I can't be I hope you are well and doing fine and and still loving me as I am loving you.

Well I hope you find Mama and Papa well and doing fine. Give them my love and tell them to keep on praying that war will be over soon so we can be together again for good. Darling if something don't soon happen I guess I'll be crazy. I miss you so until I am almost crazy now. I miss you so much. If I did not love you I would not miss you or care, but it's different. I love you and always will no matter what happens. And I hope you are the same by me darling, and I hope you will always love me as I do you. If you ever stop loving me I don't know what I will do because there is no other one in my life but you and never will be. And I hope it won't be long before we are together so I can prove myself to you. Well darling, I must close with all the kisses and love from me to you. So keep sweet and true for your true loving husband.

PFC Lee A. Turner

I love you darling.

# Flournoy and Bessie Miller

*Schomburg Center for Research in Black Culture*

Flournoy Miller (1887–1971) was an actor, comedian, playwright, lyricist, and producer. Born in Nashville, Tennessee, he began his career while attending Fisk University, where he and Aubrey Lyles, a childhood friend, formed a twenty-five-year partnership. Among the productions he worked with were the controversial *Amos and Andy* show, *Shuffle Along,* and *Sugar Hill,* collaborating with, among others, Eubie Blake and Noble Sissle. The correspondence with his wife Bessie, which was written between 1943 and 1965, is playful and suggestive.

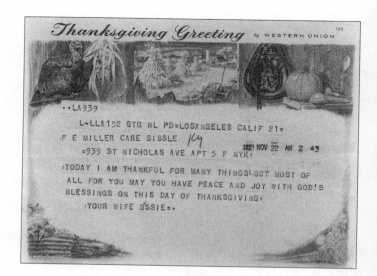

## TELEGRAM FROM BESSIE TO FLOURNOY

*Thanksgiving 1943*

TODAY I AM THANKFUL FOR MANY THINGS
BUT MOST OF ALL FOR YOU MAY YOU HAVE
PEACE AND JOY WITH GOD'S BLESSINGS ON
THIS DAY OF THANKSGIVING

YOUR WIFE BESSIE

## To Bessie from Flournoy

My Dear sweet baby

Don't think because I didn't write this evening I wasn't thinking of you for I was dear.

The only excuse I can offer is that I'm a very poor composer. But you won't be angry with me will you? For I love only you. Come home early.

Your Dady [sic]

oooooooooooooooooooooooooo
Kisses and oceans of love

## TO BESSIE FROM FLOURNOY

My own sweet baby:

Surprised aren't you? Thought I wasn't going to
write however I love you and will do anything to
please you.

Won't you be glad when we meet at home
tonight? I will. Instead of writing how I love you
I'll tell you then.

1000000000000000000000000000000 kisses
from your Dady [sic]

My Dear Sweet baby

  I will miss you so m[uch]
want you to think of me, for
had you in my arms all n[ight]
some of these days, dady.
now all to himself and we
know it, we can't help, [it]
're the happiest couple
I told Arolley and he said
anything about that never fear a
lost confidence in your
baby would'nt do any.
[illegible] love in your
[illegible]
[illegible]

My own sweet baby:

Surprised aren't you? Thought I wasn't going to write however I love you and will do anything to please you.

Won't you be glad when we meet at home tonight? I will. Instead of writing how I love you I'll tell you then.

10000000000000000000000000000000 kisses
from your Dady [sic]

my Dear Sweet baby

I will miss you so m
want you to think of me. for
had you in my arms all
some of these days. dady
you all to himself and we
know it. we can't help
're the happiest couple
I told Crolley and he said
anything about that never fear a
lost confidence in you
baby wouldn't do any
every bone in your

My Dear Sweet Baby,

I will miss you so much tonight and I want you to think of me for I will be wishing I had you in my arms all night.

Some of these days dady [sic] is going to have you all to himself and we'll let the world know it. We can't help but be happy for we're the happiest couple in the world now. I told Aubrey and he said he didn't think anything about that. Never fear dear dady [sic] has the utmost confidence in you. He knows his little baby wouldn't do anything wrong and I love every bone in your body. Time will prove to you how much I love you. Some day we will have a home and call it love cottage with lots of Flournoylets and Bessielets running around.

Be a sweet baby until dady [sic] sees you again.

  10000000000000 Kisses
  Your Dady [sic]

My own sweet baby:

You have no idea how I'll miss you but things will be arranged some day so that we wont have to be separated.

You certainly wrote me a sweet letter. The contents made me very happy. I'll do all I can to prove worthy of you. I only wish I could write a sweet letter like you. However I love you and will do all I can to prove it.

Be a sweet baby,
Your Devoted Daddy

P.S. 99 million kisses and all my love to you, the sweetest of all

## PART FIVE

# The Civil Rights Era
# to the Present

*T*HE BATTLE FOR equal rights, which has defined the entire history of African Americans in the United States, took on new meaning following a war in which so many black men had served with distinction. More and more, African Americans challenged measures denying them equal opportunity. Following the war, a series of barriers were toppled. In 1947, Jackie Robinson became the first African American baseball player in the Major Leagues, and the President's Committee on Civil Rights condemned racial injustice and advocated the elimination of segregation in American life.

The following year Ralph Bunche, a distinguished political scientist, was named temporary United Nations mediator in Palestine and was awarded the Nobel Peace Prize. In 1950, Gwendolyn Brooks became the first African American to receive a Pulitzer Prize, and a number of Supreme Court decisions, among them *Brown v. Board of*

*Education* of Topeka in 1954, found discrimination and segregation unconstitutional. In the 1960s, the Civil Rights Movement took off; Martin Luther King made great strides, dreamed dreams, only to be shot down in 1968. The struggle continued into the '70s, '80s, and '90s. At the beginning of the twenty-first century, many of the most blatant racial hurdles had fallen. But despite gains, full racial equality remains an elusive goal for many African Americans given the wide racial disparities in income, access to medical care, education attainment, arrest rates and incarceration levels fostered by generations of slavery, Jim Crow, and persistent racism. But through it all, the love shared between African Americans endures.

With the growing prevalence of e-mail, cell phones, pagers, and the like, the kinds of poetic and elegantly crafted love letters written by African Americans from the nineteenth century throughout the twentieth century may become cherished relics of a bygone era. But at least one contemporary couple still writes long, passionate letters during periods of separation. This section ends with the letters of Francesca Momplaisir and Nnabu Gogoh, who wed February 14, 2002.

# Booker T. Washington III
## and Joyce Washington

*Mrs. Washington's Personal Collection*

Booker T. Washington III (1915–1994) was the grandson of his namesake, who was one of the most influential African Americans of the twentieth century. The younger Washington was born in Tuskegee, Alabama, and in 1938 graduated from Tuskegee Institute, the school his grandfather founded, with a degree in architecture. In 1966, he went to New York, where he met Joyce, a native of Norfolk, Virginia, who had graduated from Virginia State College and received a master's degree in school administration from Hampton Institute in 1962.

The couple married in 1967 and settled in New York, where she worked as an educator and he as an architect. Mrs. Washington had served as assistant superintendent of the New York City schools and for twenty years worked as an elementary school principal. Meanwhile, her husband worked for a number of architectural firms and was involved in the planning and design of several major New

York landmarks, including the Metropolitan Opera House at Lincoln Center, the Pan Am Building, and Rockefeller University.

The letter that follows was written after they were married but while Mrs. Washington completed the school term in Norfolk, Virginia, where she worked as a school principal. She reunited with her husband in New York at the end of the school year.

*February 4, 1968*

My precious Wife—

Just a few more days and it will all be over—the waiting—aching—longing to be with you. . . .

I love you very much—and hope that this tortuous time that we are both enduring—when apart—will not weaken, demoralize or destroy our high hope for a wonderful future together.

Yours—Booker

# Monique Greenwood Pogue
## and Glenn Pogue

Greenwood (b. 1959), a native of Washington, D.C., is an author, journalist and entrepreneur who also served as editor-in-chief of *Essence* magazine. Even while running the magazine, Greenwood, along with her husband Glenn Pogue (b. 1959), continued to operate a string of successful businesses in Brooklyn, including a bed-and-breakfast, a restaurant, a bookstore, and a hair salon. They also own a bed-and-breakfast in Cape May, New Jersey.

The couple met at a party during which Glenn was so taken with Monique that he penned a letter to her on the back of the party flyer. Glenn, the son of an Army officer, lived in many cities throughout his childhood and went on to serve in the Navy. He also worked as a network broadcast engineer. The couple was married in 1989 and in 1991 had a daughter, Glynn. Greenwood is the author of *Having What Matters: The Black Woman's Guide to Creating the Life You Really Want* (William Morrow).

Monique,

Meeting you has been really great! . . . Your warmth just makes me feel oh so comfortable! . . . you've done a lot for me inspirationally! I feel as though I've just got a jolt like a jump start or something. This is really fabulous. Let's be friends Monique. I said, I find you quite attractive. . . . We'll be friends first then . . . well . . . you know what I mean. Anyway thanks again. I hope to see some? A lot? More? of you in the near future. Have a good day Monique. (Mommi)

Glenn

# Lana Turner

Lana Turner (b. 1950) is a ubiquitous fixture in Harlem, which is her home and preoccupation. The New York native is a real estate agent, professional events planner, and a Harlem bibliophile whose home is the repository for photographs, news clippings, and letters that recall Harlem's heralded history. The letters that follow were written to Ms. Turner by James L. Hicks (1915–1986), a journalist who worked at the legendary *Amsterdam News* in New York from 1955 until 1985; and by her former husband, Michael Fane (b. 1949), a security analyst whom she met while both were students in a Harlem junior high school.

Hicks, a native of Akron, Ohio, and a graduate of Howard University, was hired as managing editor of the *Amsterdam News* in 1955 and the same year was promoted to executive editor. In 1966, he was appointed commissioner with the New York State Human Rights Commission, but he returned to the *Amsterdam News* as executive editor in 1972. He left the *Amsterdam* to become executive editor of the *New York Voice* in 1978. He received a presidential citation for combat while in command of a unit in Papua, New

Guinea, and earned three battle stars for valor during the Asia Pacific Campaign.

The letters from Michael Fane were written in 1966 and 1967 after Lana's family relocated from Harlem to Florida. After a lengthy courtship, the couple married in 1969.

The letters from Hicks were written in 1982 and 1985 and map out a relationship that never quite blossomed into romance but was infused with mutual admiration.

## TO LANA FROM MICHAEL

*February 15, 1966*

Dear Lana,

. . . In your last letter you reminded me that your heart was with me. You also said to take good care of it. Well nothing will happen to it as long as we love each other. You see Miss Turner I still love you and I won't ever do anything to hurt you. Well it's that time again . . . Remember I love you.

> Your boy from
> New York City
> Michael

*October 12, 1967*

Dear Lana;

. . . my love for you grows each day. I long to be
with you. I read your letters almost everyday. I don't
write very often because I am afraid I am being
repetitious. Lana I love you and I hope you'll wait
for me.

Love Always
Your husband Michael

The next series of letters are to Lana from Jimmy Hicks, who was editor of the *Amsterdam News,* where he was later a columnist. They were written in 1982, after Lana's divorce from her husband Michael.

## To Lana from Jimmy

*Undated and typed, written around 1982*

Lana,

. . . In the bfief [sic] time that I have known you—
the brief, sweet period of YOU and ME—I have
always been painfully aware that I have always been
the aggressor—the guy waiting in the wings—
never specifically saying what he is waiting for—
but definitely, and always <u>waiting</u>.

All of that to say again, that I have always been
the agressor [sic] between YOU and ME.

And now comes the hard part:

At this point, for reasons best known to me, only,
I have decided to simply walk away from the wings
in which I have been standing and ease on down the
back stairs of the stage door and out into the streets
where I came from, and out of your life, which I
should have never so aggressively entered.

And therein lies the problem.

I want to walk away—to ease on down the road,
with your Blessings.

But does the luxury of Self Reproach give me
that right? I hope so. I have confessed to being the
agressor [sic]. But does that simple confession

permit me to suddenly walk away from the brief sweet moments we've shared without explaining why I walked away?

This is vitally important to me because I cherish every moment I've shared with you and I'd like to walk away with the feeling that you might at least feel somewhat towards me, as I most certainly feel towards you—that there was once a person I met, who was all that I could ever ask in a woman— but that time and circumstance dictated that she was not, and couldn't be, for me.

I could say much more, but it all would add up to the same thing.

Your beautiful life is already programmed and filled with the things which make for a Great Life—loyal friends, devoted family, admiring lovers—the whole bit—everything that dictates that I should simply, ease on down the road!

> Try to understand,
> Love,
> Jimmy

## To Lana from Jimmy

*Likely written in 1985*

Lady!

I refuse to blame you for the deep feelings which caused me to foolishly hope that the meeting of such a great Lady could, and would, develop into a deeper relationship.

Nor will I attempt to blame you in any way because such a relationship did not develop.

As I look back, I can see now that you were trying all the time to get such a message over to me, but I'm aggressive and it took me a long time to get it, because I was virtually blinded in my attraction for you.

I can see more clearly now, and tho the pain is not gone, I can fully understand.

I wish you and Eric all the best.

I will not try to see you again. I hope I will not see you again because the pain is too great.

Please know, however, that I will always be a concerned friend—living just outside the Great Wall which you and your busy life has placed between us.

And if there should ever come a time when you need another friend, just look beyond the wall and I'll be there to help.

Good luck on the road ahead,

Jimmy

# Derrick Bell and
# Janet Dewart Bell

Derrick Bell (b. 1931) is a lawyer, activist, best-selling author, and scholar who gained national prominence in 1992 when he sacrificed his tenured position at Harvard University Law School to protest the school's failure to grant tenure to women of color. He has continued to write and to teach at New York University Law School. Among his many books are *Faces at the Bottom of the Well* and *Confronting Authority,* which chronicles his protest at Harvard.

Bell, a native of Pittsburgh who grew up in a working-class family, attended the University of Pittsburgh Law School, where he edited the law review. Upon graduating, he worked for the Justice Department's Civil Rights Division and then became executive director of the Pittsburgh branch of the NAACP. He joined the Harvard Law faculty in 1969.

For thirty years, Bell was married to his best friend, Jewel, who succumbed to breast cancer in 1990. That same year he met Janet Dewart, a public relations practitioner who was editing the National Urban League's annual *The*

*State of Black America* report. Dewart wanted to include one of Bell's fictional stories in the volume of essays. For several weeks the two engaged in lengthy telephone conversations. They finally met in January 1991, by which time Janet was already in love. Bell wrote the following passages to Janet in May of 1991 out of concern for her deepening involvement with him and his own uncertainty about his feelings so soon after his wife's passing. The couple married in June 1992.

## TO JANET FROM DERRICK

*Undated*

Janet,

The essence of Spring is not new life, but that
risk of death—assumed eagerly by those first
blossoms eagerly offering proof of Winter's end.
They break forth, more bravely than wisely into
weather more likely still freezing than graced
with unseasonly warmth. Despite what may
prove a fatal chill, they stand. Proud sentinels
on watch for a spring they herald but may
never see.

My love is as one with these first blooms.
Beautiful and yet far too fragile to face the
blustery winds that symbolize season's change.
How honor courage that is its own reward?
How protect those who value heart-shaped
duty over safety?

Whether fortuity or fate, those first flowers
burst forth too soon reminding a waiting world to
look beyond blowing snow toward waving fields of
bee-filled blooms: the more fortunate but no more
noble successors to these first few.

There is parallel but no protection for a heart
too filled with love to wait its season that might

never come. She stands there in an uncertain climate and, like the early blooms, relies on an inner warmth, responding to an older rhythm than logic, and relishing in the simple glory of risk.

DB

# Francesca Momplaisir
and Nnabu Gogoh

Francesca Momplaisir (b. 1973), a native of Haiti who came
to the United States at age two, was raised in Queens, New
York, where she early on developed her gift for writing.
Her poetry and short stories helped earn her a number of
prizes and honors, and in 1994, while a student at New

York University, she was named one of *Glamour* magazine's top ten students; *USA Today*'s Top 20 students; and received early induction into Phi Beta Kappa. She graduated magna cum laude from New York University in 1995 and was valedictorian for her class. She attended Columbia University and Oxford University, receiving master's degrees in English, and then enrolled in New York University's doctoral program, which she plans to complete by 2003.

Momplaisir met Nnabu Gogoh (b. 1970), a first-generation American whose family hails from Africa, during an NAACP Youth Council event when Momplaisir was seventeen and in high school and Nnabu was twenty and in his sophomore year in college. The two became romantically involved several years later and after a period apart, reunited. The sweethearts married on Valentine's Day 2002. Their letters reveal a deeply passionate relationship.

## To Nnabu from Francesca

*Saturday May 8, 1999*

Hello, my love. I hope you're feeling a little better. I just received your letter dated May 5th. And yes, I am smiling from ear to ear once again. I have to stop reading so that I don't feel overwhelmed. I love you so much and I am as fortunate as you are to be in this relationship. Loving you comes quite naturally. I couldn't stop myself if I tried. You'll probably receive this along with the xeroxes from the Bible and the photograph. It's blurry, I know, but it's a copy of a copy. I took pictures today and they would be ready by Wednesday, so you'll have something clearer and more recent. When you return, we will take pictures together and you *will* smile.

I am looking forward to your return so that I can finally get a good night's sleep. No matter how early I go to bed, I wake up feeling tired partly because I wake up in the middle of the night wanting you and thinking about you. You are so important to me. I value you so much. I'm still smiling because of your letter. I'm so glad that you chose to be so expressive in writing. Yesterday I opened a fortune cookie that said, "You will be married within a year". I hope that that's the case. Actually, I know that that will be the case.

I wish that you had told me sooner how you felt

about me all these years. It would have kept me from feeling that I was insane or obsessed with you. For a long time I didn't know that you felt the same for me and I just figured that I should give it up or cover up my feelings for you because nothing was going to come of it. Even if we couldn't get together back then, I still would have liked to know what you were thinking. There were times when I thought that you really didn't love me, or didn't love me enough. I questioned myself for a long time and tried to determine what was wrong with me that kept you from loving me. I wanted your love and acceptance so much that it's sometimes hard to believe that we are where we are in this relationship. I used to have what I referred to as "Gogoh cravings". There were times when I wanted to be with you so badly it was overwhelming. I remember being with someone (in the biblical sense) years ago and hearing myself in my mind just calling out to you. I could have killed that man for not being you.

Isn't it wonderful when things fall into place and come together. When I'm with you and when reading your letters I know that this was worth waiting for. You're the one, baby. If not for situations like these with you being away, I think we'd be living a fairytale. I guess we need something to keep us grounded. I could think of other, less painful ways of keeping us from getting outlandishly euphoric, but this is the method that has been chosen for us. But, our "happily ever after" is yet to come. The stories we'll be able to tell. Our grandchildren or great grandchildren will someday discover our letters in an old attic covered with dust and read them and know that they are the products of an incredible love. I'm so happy to be loved by you. Now all we need to do is get you back home.

I just need to see you and touch you and really know that you're okay. D.C. sent me an email asking me in jest when you and I are planning to get married. He didn't expect me to have a timeframe so soon. I often think that if I had been in his shoes I would have let go a long time ago, years ago. If I knew that my mate had such strong feelings for someone else, I could never stay. I really believe that we all have "one true love". That's not to say that we can't love other people and be happy with them. But, at some point in our lives, usually early on, we all encounter one individual who is our one true love. I think that very few people actually end up with that person. I'm very fortunate to have that come back to me.

> I love you, sweetie.
> Francesca

*Saturday June 12, 1999*

Hello There, Love. It's been so long since I've actually written you from home that it makes me smile to be able to look at your picture as I write to you. Sometimes I'm almost afraid to look at your picture for fear that it will make me miss you more than I already do. It's almost heartbreaking. The only way that you could possibly understand the depth and breadth of my love for you is if you love me the same way that I do. I believe that you do. So, next time, before you question yourself about my love for you, think of how much you love me and know that I love you equally. Isn't it wonderful to feel like this? I was just watching a show called "Mepteres of the Bible" on A&E and they were discussing the Bible's position on romantic love and sex. As they were discussing true love, the passion and the commitment that is required to decide to spend your entire life with another person a smile came to my face and I thought of you. I was also watching another show on which the "husband" hugged his "wife" and the actor let slip this smile that was so much like your smile after we've embraced. It was so genuine and so reminiscent of your uncensored pleasure of being with me. I do believe that you love me.

I can actually feel my love for you physically. I have a visceral reaction to thoughts of you, the sight of you and the sound of your voice. I can actually feel my breast contract as I write to you right now. Sometimes it raises a lump in my throat and I am near tears of joy because of the love that I feel for you and that I know you feel for me!. . . I love you more than anything, baby.

*February 2, 2000*

. . . I am so fortunate to be in love with you. It's a gratifying feeling to be able to look within myself and find you there and find that love there. Sometimes, when I'm taking my mental and emotional temperature, I reach inside almost physically to let myself feel everything that is occurring inside. I love the feeling I get when I think about you. I love knowing that that love is alive within, that it has a real target, that it's you, that you are alive and healthy and in my life. I love it. I love knowing that there is a future for us even if we cannot see it. I know that it is there, somewhere in front of us, in time.

. . . A couple of weeks ago when I visited you, we locked eyes for a moment. I don't know if you felt it. Actually, I do know that you felt it. I'm just not sure that you remember it. We were held in each other's gaze and I could feel you, touching me through the glass. I could feel you. . . . It was so powerful that I couldn't hold my eyes in yours like for an extended period. That confirmed for me that what we have is beyond powerful and that it is indestructible, it is perpetual. This thing of ours is forever. You are my husband. We mate for life.

Forever Yours,
Francesca

*February 18, 2000*

Hey You,

How are you? I been in need of my baby something awful lately. I miss you so very much. Always remember that I love you and will always be in love with you.

Sometimes I feel so inadequate when writing to you. I feel as though there should always be something extremely profound to communicate to you yet when I re-read my words to you I realize that the most profound thing that I can say to you is just that I love you. Isn't life wonderful sometimes. Thank you for simple pleasures. I cannot believe how far I've come in terms of my expression of love for you. Never have I been so free in giving and receiving love. Only true love can enable a person such as myself to let such changes occur. See what you made me do? I'm turning into a sensitive, corny ball of mush. And I love it!

Yours forever,
Sweetie

## To Francesca from Nnabu

*February 20, 2000*

My Love,

... I love you more each day. At first, I didn't think it were possible. When moments like that occur, that is usually when we have one of our conversations that awaken some dormant or non-existent part of me or I receive a letter much like the one this morning and then it happens. Somehow there always seems to be a deeper sense of belonging left over. As if we were living in an oversized mansion with so many unopened rooms that only increase our love for our home, our home. I feel so complete being with you, having you for my own.

Sometimes I wish that I could just tuck you away somewhere deep inside of me so that we would always be together. Is that the epitome of selfishness or what? However, I realize that in order for us to grow as a unit, we each need to grow as individuals. Similar to our first separation. I hope and pray that you use your gift to the best of your capabilities and relish the day when the world will be able to recognize you for what I've always known you to be, a literary genius. Not a prodigy, but a genius.

## To Francesca from Nnabu

*March 10, 2000*

Francesca,

My dear sweet woman, when can I possibly begin to describe my feelings for you? All I seem to do is contemplate what life, our life together will bring. And it comes so easily. This is the one area in which I can conjure up extremely vivid scenes. I see us as mirror images of one another, each being totally free with and within the other. Does that make sense?

For as much as I can't wait to come home to you, I am scared almost petrified. There are times when I wonder if your feelings towards me will change somehow or if you will realize that our separation only heightened what we felt just before my departure. Deep within my soul I know it won't happen so please forgive me for seemingly doubting your devotion to me. I won't even touch the topic of fidelity.

In your letter I discovered how in tune you are to me and my emotional state. You wrote "you were just discovering your happiness". How exact, how precise, it's almost frightening. Up until now I couldn't properly describe just what I was experiencing back then and in one full swoop of the pen (or stroke of the keyboard) you managed to pinpoint my emotion. How dare you know me so well. I love you. I can recall sitting on the passenger seat on that "neon" Neon that you had rented to go to PA. (Not knowing just how many more trips you would be making to PA.) I would look over at you sometimes and wonder how I could be or rather feel so complete with a woman. (Not that I've been complete with a man! Ha ha!) I was and am still not in want of anything. Only when one finds their true partner, their soul mate, can this plane of existence be reached. You touch me in places that were long since buried and forgotten.

I'm gradually coming to accept this situation for what it is, temporary. Similar to the years that we spent apart, I learned that those years helped me to really enjoy our reunion. So following the same rationale, this time away will do the same only on a more permanent level upon my return.

Our first date will be a long walk to the "SWPP" (secret white people's park). All I want is to be alone with you, free from the company of people and their chatter. I want to hold you close to me while we walk through the park. I want to take you home, draw us a hot bath, rub you down, and lay you to sleep in my arms (cheap date huh). Although we always have something to talk about, I appreciated the times when our souls communicate to one another. Those times when we lay down and instinctively mesh into the perfect sleeping position, the times when a glance relays a message that words couldn't begin to express. In you I've found myself, and in us I've found the future. I hope and pray that the first few months of our reuniting were only a prelude to the years of happiness to follow.

Forever your sweetie,
Nnabu

*June 6, 2000*

Hey you,

. . . Discussing anything other than us seems so burdensome, so trivial. I love Francesca. So very much. Maybe when I return to you, we can lock ourselves away, whether here or in Nigeria, and just be together. I miss holding you close to me. I miss sniffing at your neck, putting my head on your breast. I miss everything about you, about us. One day soon we will pick up where we left off. I love you to no end.

*June 10, 2000*

Hey You—

How's my baby doing? I have to tell you that it
hurts not to see you this weekend. Even though
it's my own idea that you not come, I still feel the
pinch of wanting to see you and not being able to.
Sometimes I wonder just why it is that I punish
myself. Lord only knows that if I had my way I
would be with you every waking moment. I love to
finish your sentences, I love to say "bless you" when
you sneeze. I love to look into your eyes and make
you blush. I just love you.

Although talking to you seems more personal,
I feel as if I'm better able to express my feelings for
you in writing a little more clearly. Through you, I
am able to see my future and unlock my potential.
Because you love me I am able to return that love
to you in ways that often surprise me. With you, I
hope to be a part of a family, eternally bound by
love and mutual admiration.

Even though you don't like to hear this, I will
continue to thank you not only for your love, but
also for your friendship. This friendship, built over

the years on long conversations, arranged meetings and failed relationships, has not only strengthened our bond, but has given us the rare opportunity, often denied most, to try again. For your support, both from near and far, I am now and will always be eternally grateful. Just grin and bear the compliments. You are more than deserving of them and more. I promise to forever hold you dear to my heart and commit myself totally to loving you.

Forever Yours,

## To Francesca from Nnabu

*September 28, 2000*

Hey you,

I got your letter this morning and you would not
like my reaction. It's been so long since I've smelled
your perfume that I had to put your letter away for
quite some time. I placed it under my pillow and
cried myself back to sleep. I haven't had such a
physical reaction to anything in quite a long time.
It's amazing how much emotion can be contained in
a scent. (I'm still shaking as I write this letter.)
. . . Being with you makes me proud and
confident. I know that when we are together, you
are with me and I with you. There is no insecurity,
no question as to where your heart lies. I have never
experienced that with anyone other than you. When
I smile, it's genuine; when I express my feelings to
you, it's effortless; and when we embrace and make
love, it's complete. There isn't any other way to
explain it. . . . I love you, Francesca, That's it. There
is nothing else to say.

Always Yours.
Nnabu Sweetie

# Tim and Daphne Reid

The Reids met in the early 1970s in Chicago, where they worked with the same talent agency for modeling and commercials. While each knew who the other was, they led separate lives and were married to other people. In 1980, they were reacquainted in Los Angeles, where they had both gone to pursue their careers. By then both were divorced and in hot pursuit of their acting careers. They exchanged phone calls and met for a drink that was to have lasted five minutes, but lasted five hours and into breakfast. "We haven't been apart from that day until this," Daphne recalls.

The couple, who have both had successful acting careers and paired up in the critically acclaimed *Frank's Place* television series in the 1990s, married in December of 1982. "It's been the twenty-year ride of a lifetime," says Daphne, "full of hard work, love, and laughter."

## A Love Poem to Daphne from Tim

*Written in 1980*

As romance leads you through its narrow path,
Your face shows that of fear.
Your passionate sigh is often cut short
By customary doubt.
I see that need for control
Hidden behind that soft smile.
You're falling in love, you say.
Your touch at times is more like a gentle probe,
As you quench that tremendous need
To know me. Yet I wish your need
Was just to feel me. But I understand,
You're falling in love, you say.
I too have felt that apprehension that only
Lovers feel as we stand before love's throne.
What will it be this time—freedom or slavery?
Will you suffer the pains of separation
Or the joys of growth?
The only sure thing is . . .
You're falling in love, you say.
Your heart follows its exterior lead as your
Mind struggles to assert its egotistical needs.
All this confusion just because life's led you to me.
And what about me? Is this "me" feeling the same?
After all, this is serious . . .
I'm falling in love you say